What Do You Know
About Tibet
Questions and Answers

Compiled by: Wang Chen   Dong Yunhu

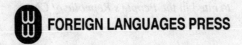
FOREIGN LANGUAGES PRESS

First Edition 2011

Second Printing 2011

ISBN 978-7-119- 07015-5

© Foreign Languages Press Co. Ltd, Beijing, China, 2011

Published by Foreign Languages Press Co. Ltd

24 Baiwanzhuang Road, Beijing 100037, China

http://www.flp.com.cn   E-mail: flp@cipg.org.cn

Distributed by China International Book Trading Corporation

35 Chegongzhuang Xilu, Beijing 100044, China

P.O. Box 399, Beijing, China

Contents

II. The Question of Sovereignty

III. Human Rights

IV. Regional Ethnic Autonomy

V. Development of Economy and Society

VI. Religious Beliefs

VII. Culture, Education and Medical Services

VIII. Protection of the Ecological Environment

IX. Questions Concerning the Dalai Lama

X. The Violence in Lhasa on March 14, 2008

Preface

China is a united multi-ethnic country with a vast territory and a huge population. People living in any parts of this land are eager to see the beauty of other parts of China and to know their fellow-countrymen living there. In recent years the world has been showing growing interest in Tibet – the "Roof of the World" – for its extraordinary beauty and culture. The world wants to know about Tibet.

In order to provide a window on Tibet, the Information Office of the State Council pooled the wisdom of experienced scholars and experts on the study of Tibet, as well as professionals who serve Tibet for years. The team spent several years soliciting questions from readers with various interests. It finally picked 147 questions, classified them into ten categories and answered them in an easy-to-understand way.

What Do You Know About Tibet? Questions and Answers contains general knowledge of topics of interest as well as controversial issues. No sharp question is avoided. This book seeks accuracy, and bases its arguments on historical materials, facts and statistics. It adopts the popular and simple Q&A form, and the answers are brief and to the point.

Ten aspects are covered – Tibet's administration and history, question of sovereignty, human rights, regional ethnic autonomy, development of economy and society, religious beliefs, culture, education and medical services, protection of the ecological environment, questions concerning the Dalai Lama, and the violence in Lhasa on March 14, 2008. The answers reflect the current development of Tibet and the latest situation of Tibet-related issues, basically reflecting the central government's stand.

In compiling this book, the Information Office of the State Council organized experts from the China Tibetology Research Center and China International Publishing Group to discuss and revise the manuscript several times. The consultants adjusted the content, and checked the chapter arrangement, historical facts and statistics of the book.

We have done our best to provide comprehensive coverage of the Tibet-related questions of most interest to readers all over the world, and hope they will find it helpful.

Editor
March 1, 2011

Administration
and History

1. Where does the name Tibet come from?

The word "Xizang" (or "Tibet") refers to the Tibet Autonomous Region of the People's Republic of China.

Tibet was known by many different names in history, such as "Tubo" in the Tang Dynasty (618-907), "Xibo" in the Song Dynasty (960-1127), the "Ü, Tsang and Ngari Korsum area" in the Yuan Dynasty (1127-1368), and "Ü-Tsang" in the Ming (1368-1644) and Qing (1644-1911) dynasties. The word "Xizang" appeared in 1663, or the second year of Qing Emperor Kangxi's reign (1622-1722).

In the mid-Yuan Dynasty Tibet was officially brought within the jurisdiction of China's central government. The central government fostered Sakya sect of Tibetan Buddhism and helped it establish a local political regime to govern the Tibetan region, and set up a number of local military and administrative organs on the Qinghai-Tibet Plateau. The Yuan's founding emperor Kublai Khan divided the plateau into three administrative areas, Amdo, Do-kham and Ü-Tsang. During Qing Emperor Kangxi's reign the Tibetan areas ruled by the Dalai Lama and the Panchen Erdeni were referred to by their traditional names of Ü-Tsang and Tubbat. Later, the name "Ü-Tsang" evolved into "Xizang."

The name "Xizang" first appeared in the *Annals of the Qing Dynasty*, which contains a 1663 record that "Xizang's Panchen Erdeni Hutuktu passed away and court officials were sent to his funeral." In 1721 Qing government troops dispelled the Dzungar Mongols. Emperor Kangxi composed the inscription on the stele commemorating the pacification of Xizang, which officially gave the name "Xizang" to the Ü-Tsang region.

Xizang's English equivalent "Tibet" probably came from the word "Tubbat," which was used by the Turkic and Mongol peoples to call the people of Tibet. In terms of ethnic group, "Tibet" is related to the Tibetan people. In terms of geography, "Tibet" could refer to the Tibet Autonomous Region or the Tibetan region, meaning the whole area inhabited by the Tibetan people. Therefore, "Tibet" is not fully equal to the modern Chinese word "Xizang."

2. Both the terms "Tibet" and "the Tibetan region" can often be seen in publications. Is there any difference between them? Has a unified "Greater Tibet" ever existed in history?

"Tibet" refers to the Tibet Autonomous Region of the People's Republic of China. The region comprises six prefectures – Nyingchi, Chamdo, Shannan, Shigatse, Nagchu and Ngari, and the regional capital city of Lhasa, under which there are a total of 74 counties, including a city district, a county-level city and a special administrative district. The counties consist of 690 townships. Tibet covers an area of over 1.2 million sq km.

Songtsen Gampo (?-650) founded the Tubo kingdom in the region, which was known as "Ü-Tsang" during the Yuan Dynasty. From an edict issued by Qing Emperor Kangxi mentioning "Tibet's Panchen Erdeni Hutuktu," the region received its name Tibet, which is still in use today.

The Tibetan region is a comprehensive reference to the Tibetan autonomous divisions set up in accordance with China's Constitution and Law on Regional Ethnic Autonomy. The region includes the Tibet Autonomous Region, Qinghai Province's Haibei, Huangnan, Hainan, Golog and Yushu Tibetan autonomous prefectures and Haixi Mongol-Tibetan Autonomous Prefecture, Gansu Province's Gannan Tibetan Autonomous Prefecture and

Tianzhu Tibetan Autonomous County, Sichuan Province's Ngapa Tibetan-Qiang Autonomous Prefecture, Garze Tibetan Autonomous Prefecture and Muli Tibetan Autonomous County, and Yunnan Province's Dechen Tibetan Autonomous Prefecture.

"Tibet" and "the Tibetan region" are different, yet related, expressions.

The Dalai Lama and his followers intentionally use the English word "Tibet" as an equivalent to "the Tibetan region" for the purpose of advocating his idea of a "Greater Tibet" and promoting "Tibetan independence."

The distribution pattern and administrative division of the Tibetan population was formed over a long historical process of development. There has never been any historical precedent for the administrative concept of "Greater Tibet." The Dalai Lama's so-call "Greater Tibet" covers 2.4 million sq km, about one quarter of China's total territory. In fact, the Tibetan-inhabited areas included in his idea of a "Greater Tibet" have never formed a unified administrative and economic region since the Tubo kingdom collapsed. Furthermore, the former local government of Tibet never governed other Tibetan-inhabited areas outside Tibet. Therefore, a unified "Greater Tibet" has never existed in history.

3. What are Tibet's current administrative divisions? How were these divisions formed?

Located in China's southwest border area, the Tibet Autonomous Region covers an area of over 1.2 million sq km. The region is composed of the regional capital city of Lhasa and six autonomous prefectures – Shigatse, Shannan, Chamdo, Nagchu, Ngari and Nyingchi. According to 2007 statistics, these divisions administer a total of 74 counties, including a city district, a county-level city and a special administrative district, and the counties consist of 690 townships.

City/Prefecture	Counties (city district/county-level city/special administrative district) under its jurisdiction
Lhasa (1 district and 7 counties)	Chengguan District and Medrogungkar, Taktse, Tohlung Dechen, Chushur, Nyemo, Damshung and Lhundrup counties
Shigatse (1 city and 17 counties)	Shigatse City and Namling, Dingri, Gyantse, Panam, Sakya, Lhatse, Nnangring, Dromo, Rinpung, Nyelam, Khangmar, Dingkye, Kyirong, Saga, Gampa, Shetongmon and Drongpa counties
Shannan (12 counties)	Nedong, Gongkar, Luntse, Nakartse, Chongye, Sangri, Chusum, Tsomey, Dranang, Lhodrak, Gyatsa and Tsona counties
Chamdo (11 counties)	Chamdo, Markham, Jomda, Gonjo, Tengchen, Traya, Zogang, Riwoche, Pashod, Lhorong and Palbar counties
Nagchu (1 special administrative district and 10 counties)	Tsonyi special administrative district and Nagchu, Shantsa, Amdo, Driru, Palgon, Bachen, Lhari, Nyanrong, Nyima and Sog counties

Ngari (7 counties)	Purang, Gar, Gegye, Gertse, Tsochen, Zada and Rutok counties
Nyingchi (7 counties)	Nyingchi, Kongpo Gyamda, Menling, Pome, Zayul, Metok and Nang counties

Tibet was known by many different names in history, such as "Tubo" in the Tang Dynasty (618-907), "Xibo" in the Song Dynasty (960-1127), the "Ü, Tsang and Ngari Korsum area" in the Yuan Dynasty (1127-1368), and "Ü-Tsang" in the Ming (1368-1644) and Qing (1644-1911) dynasties. The word "Xizang" appeared in 1663, or the second year of Qing Emperor Kangxi's reign (1622-1722).

The Tubo kingdom established the first administrative units on the Tibetan Plateau. In its early period the Tubo kingdom was divided into four "*ru*" (wings), and 61 "*tongdai*" (a unit consisting of a thousand households). The four *ru* were the Ü *ru* (central wing) with Lhasa at the center, Yo *ru* (left wing) with Nedong at the center, Ye *ru* (right wing) with Namling at the center, and Rulag (branch wing) with Lhatse at the center. The *ru* roughly covered the basins of the Yarlung Tsangpo River and its tributaries, including the Lhasa, Nyakchu and Nyangchu rivers. Later, the administrative division "Sumpa *ru*" was set up in northern Tibet and at the foot of the Tanggula Mountains.

During the nearly 400 years that followed the collapse of the Tubo kingdom in the 9th century, the various tribes in the region established separate regimes on the Tibetan Plateau.

In the mid-13th century the Yuan central government put the entire Qinghai-Tibet Plateau under the direct jurisdiction of Xuanzheng Yuan or the Ministry of Tibetan Governance. Three High Pacification Commissioner's Offices, a kind of provincial-level administrative division, were set up under the ministry to handle Tibetan affairs. During the Yuan Dynasty the area of today's Tibet Autonomous Region was administered by the Do-kham and Ü-Tsang High Pacification Commissioner's Offices.

The Ming central government maintained most of the Yuan administrative divisions in the above-mentioned areas. Under Ming rule, the area of today's Tibet Autonomous Region was at first administered by the Ü-Tsang Garrison and the Do-kham Garrison, which were later upgraded to two Itinerant High Commanderies. The jurisdiction area of the Ming Dynasty's Ü-Tsang Itinerant High Commandery was approximately equal to that of the Yuan Dynasty's Ü-Tsang High Pacification Commissioner's Office. In the western part of the Ü-Tsang area the Ming government set up the E-Li-Si Army-Civilian Marshal's Office to govern the area that is now called Ngari and the territory to the west of Ngari. The jurisdiction area of the Ming Dynasty's Do-kham Itinerant High Commandery was roughly equal to that of the Yuan Dynasty's Do-kham High Pacification Commissioner's Office, and there were only slight changes. Both the two Itinerant High Commanderies had subordinate administrative organs, including commanderies, pacification commissioner's offices, amnesty and expedition commissioners, *wanhu* offices (myri-archies, each in command of 10,000 households), and *qianhu* offices (chiliarchies, each in command of 1,000 households) to exercise direct rule over the Tibetan people.

On the basis of the Ming administrative establishments in Tibet, the Qing central government made detailed adjustments to administrative divisions in Tibet and the boundary areas between Tibet and its neighboring provinces in the 1720s. The Qing central government first surveyed and determined the geographical boundaries between Sichuan Province and Tibet, and between Yunnan Province and Tibet. Then it moved the 79 tribes living in the eastern part of northern Tibet to the region south of the headwaters of the Yellow River under the jurisdic-tion of the high commissioners stationed in Tibet and Qinghai. The area inhabited by the 39 Sogu tribes was placed under the direct jurisdiction of the high commissioner stationed in Tibet. Besides, the Qing central government delimited the jurisdiction areas for the Dalai Lama and the Panchen Erdeni. By then, the Qing administrative divisions in Tibet were composed of areas under the jurisdiction of the Dalai Lama, the Panchen Erdeni, the direct jurisdiction of the high commissioners, and fiefdoms under the jurisdiction of the high commissioners.

In 1906 the Qing central government decided to establish the provincial-level Special Administrative Region of the Sichuan-Yunnan Borders. From 1908 to 1911 the Qing government set up administrative offices in today's Kongpo Gyamda, Lhari, Riwoche, Traya, Chamdo, Jomda, Lhorong, Markham, Gonjo and Zayul in succession, and Dengke Prefecture in today's Derge in the Garze Tibetan Autonomous Prefecture, Sichuan, to supervise these offices. Though aborted since the Chinese bourgeois democratic Revolution of 1911 broke out, the Qing plan to set up Chamdo, Taizhao and Lhari prefectures marked the first sign of establishing a province in Kham.

In the early years of the Republic of China (1912-1949), instigated by the British imperialists, Tibet's local Gaxag government under the jurisdiction of the Dalai Lama sent armed forces to expel the Qing high commissioners and troops stationed in Tibet with armed force and seized areas under the direct jurisdiction of the high commissioners. The Gaxag's forces also rolled into Chambo and other places administered by the garrison commander of the Sichuan border stationed by the central government of the Republic of China as well as the area under the jurisdiction of the Dalai Lama. The British imperialists "mediated" a settlement to temporarily place 13 Tibetan counties, including Chamdo, Riwoche and Traya, under the jurisdiction of Tibet. By then, the area administered by the local Gaxag government of Tibet covered all of today's Tibet Autonomous Region, the largest Tibetan-ruled area since the Tubo kingdom disintegrated over 1,200 years ago.

From the collapse of the Tubo kingdom to the official incorporation of Tibet into the territory of China's Yuan Dynasty, no unified local regime appeared on the Tibetan Plateau. During the rule of the central governments of the Yuan, Ming and Qing dynasties, a number of regimes under names such as Sakya, Phagdru and Tsangpa once existed on the plateau. The areas they ruled differed, each being only part of today's Tibet. Although the Tibetan local Gaxag government, also known by the name Ganden Potrang, spared no effort to expand its authority after the 1911 Revolution it did not reach east of the Jinsha River or the southern foot of the Tanggula Mountains. Historical facts have proved that "Greater Tibet" and "independent Tibet" vigorously advocated by the Dalai Lama never existed.

In the 1950s Tibet experienced a period marked by three distinct coexisting political structures, namely, the local Gaxag government, the People's Liberation Committee of Chamdo and the Panchen Khenpo Assembly Committee. Following the liberation of Chamdo in October 1950, the People's Liberation Committee of Chamdo and the people's liberation committees of counties under the prefecture were officially established and directly led by the Government Administration Council of the People's Republic of China. On May 23, 1951 the Agreement Between the Central People's Government and the Local Government of Tibet on Measures for the Peaceful Liberation of Tibet, also known as the 17-Article Agreement, was signed in Beijing. According to the Agreement, Tibet was peacefully liberated, and the original status, including the jurisdiction area, of the Panchen Erdeni was restored. The existing administrative system and divisions of the Tibetan local government would not change. On April 22, 1956 the Preparatory Committee for the Tibet Autonomous Region, a consultative organ with the nature of political power, was established in Lhasa. Under the leadership of the State Council of the People's Republic of China, the three coexisting political structures still retained certain administrative powers of their own. In March 1959 the reactionary clique of the upper social strata in Tibet publicly declared "Tibet independence," and launched a full-scale armed rebellion against the central government. On March 28 the same year the State Council announced the dismissal of the former local government of Tibet, and empowered the Preparatory Committee for the Tibet Autonomous Region to exercise the functions and powers of the local government of Tibet. On April 20, 1959 the State Council removed the People's Liberation Committee of Chamdo, and on July 9, 1961 the State Council agreed to disband the Panchen Khenpo Assembly Committee upon its request and empowered the Preparatory Committee for the Tibet Autonomous Region to administer the area originally under its jurisdiction.

In January 1960, with the approval of the State Council, the Preparatory Committee for the Tibet Autonomous Region re-divided the former 83 *dzong* and 64 *dzong*-level *shika* into one city district and 72 counties, and set up seven prefectures and one city. These arrangements set up the basic framework for to-day's administrative system of the Tibet Autonomous Region.

4. How have China's central governments throughout history administered Tibet affairs?

Tibet has been part of China since ancient times. In the 13th century Tibet was officially incorporated into the territory of China's Yuan Dynasty. The Yuan central government set up 13 *wanhu* offices (myriarchies, each in command of 10,000 households) in Tibet and three High Pacification Commissioners' Offices, including the High Pacification Commissioner's Office of the Ü, Tsang and Ngari Korsum Area (the Ü-Tsang Area for short) to administer the 13 offices.

The Ming Dynasty followed the Yuan's policy of expanding the number of posts, titles and offices in Tibet. Many administrative organs, such as high commanderies, were set up and their chief officials were all appointed by the Ming central government.

The Qing Dynasty further strengthened the central government's administration of Tibet. The Qing emperors established the honorific titles of the Dalai Lama and Panchen Erdeni, set up the Department of Mongolian and Tibetan Affairs, and stationed high commissioners in Tibet. After repelling attacks by the Gurkhas (living in today's Nepal), the Qing central government promulgated the Authorized Regulations for Better Governance of Tibet, establishing a sound legal system for the administration of the region.

The Republic of China (1912-1949) declared itself a unified republic of the Han, Manchu, Mongol, Hui and Tibetan ethnic groups, and maintained its sovereignty over Tibet. The Bureau of Mongolian and Tibetan Affairs and the Commission for Mongolian and Tibetan Affairs were established by the central government to exercise jurisdiction over Tibet. The central government continued to grant honorific titles to the Dalai Lama and Panchen Erderni, and supervise the reincarnation and installation ceremonies for them.

After the founding of the People's Republic of China the central government and the local government of Tibet signed the 17-Article Agreement. In accordance with the Agreement, Tibet was liberated peacefully. In 1959 the aristocratic conservative forces staged an armed rebellion, and publicly declared "Tibet independence." After quelling the rebellion, the central government disbanded the former local government of Tibet, and carried out democratic reform in the region. The Tibet Autonomous Region was established in 1965. Thereafter, the region began to practice regional ethnic autonomy in accordance with the Constitution and related laws, regulations and policies, and implement the policies regarding ethnic groups, religions and the united front of the Communist Party of China (CPC).

5. How was the system of the Dalai Lama's administration of Tibet's local affairs formed? What was his jurisdiction area?

The Dalai Lama is one of the two leading incarnation hierarchies of Tibetan Buddhism's Gelug Sect. The title was first conferred on the 3rd Dalai Lama, but its influence and exalted position came from the continuous appointment and vigorous support from China's central governments since the early Qing Dynasty.

In 1542 the 2nd Dalai Lama Gendun Gyatso passed away, and the Drepung Monastery looked for the child who would be his reincarnation. This marked the official beginning of the reincarnation system used by the Gelug sect for leadership succession. In 1544 Drepung Monastery recognized an aristocratic boy named Sonam Gyatso as the reincarnation of Gendun Gyatso, and held an installation ceremony. Hence the boy was called a "living Buddha."

Sonam Gyatso was born at a time of great turbulence in Tibetan society. The feudal aristocratic families were engaged in fierce power struggles and continuous regime changes. The Phagdru family, which had supported the Gelug sect had long since fallen apart. The other families all supported the Karma Kagyu sect and attacked the Gelug sect in attempts to marginalize the tradition. Under such circumstances, powerful allies and backers were crucial for the survival and development of the Gelug tradition.

In 1578 Sonam Gyatso met Altan Khan, ruler of the Tumed Mongols, at Chapuqiyal (Yanghua) Temple on the southern bank of Kokonor (today's Qinghai Lake). Altan Khan conferred on Sonam Gyatso the honorific title of "All-knowing Vajradhara, His Holiness the Dalai Lama," which means that Sonam Gyatso had achieved supreme accomplishments in both exoteric and esoteric teachings and become a transcendent master whose learning was as profound and immense as the ocean. That is the origin of the Dalai Lama's title. Sonam Gyatso conferred on Altan Khan the honorific title of "Chakravartin Sechen Khan," which means that Altan Khan was a king as wise as Chakravatin (Sanskrit for "wheel turner"). Since then, with the support of the Mongol aristocrats, the Gelug sect established its power in Tibet.

According to the Gelug tradition, Sonam Gyatso was the first officially recognized Dalai Lama. The title was retrospectively given to his two predecessors, making Gendun Gyatso the second Dalai Lama and Gendun Druppa the first Dalai Lama. The Living Buddha system has been preserved to this day for over 400 years and a total of 14 lamas have borne the title.

After the third Dalai Lama passed away, his successor was born into the family of Altan Khan's oldest grandson, and was known as Yonten Gyatso, the fourth Dalai Lama. It was the first time that a Dalai Lama had been born into a Mongol royal family. In view of the political, military and religious situation of Tibet, that was probably the best choice for both the Gelug leaders and the Mongol rulers.

In 1652 the fifth Dalai Lama, Ngawang Lobsang Gyatso, was summoned to pay tribute to Qing Emperor Shunzhi (r. 1644-1661) in Beijing. The emperor conferred on him the title of "Dalai Lama, All-knowing Vajradhara, Overseer of the Buddhist Faith on Earth under the Great Benevolent Self-Existing Buddha of the Western Paradise." For the first time, a Dalai Lama was granted a gold seal and gold imperial edict issued by China's imperial house. The Dalai Lama was thereby exalted to an unprecedented status in the Gelug sect.

In 1751 the Qing Dynasty officially appointed the seventh Dalai Lama, Kelzang Gyatso, to be in charge of the Tibetan local government. The emperor abolished the position of Regent, and set up the Gaxag government with four Kalons assisting the Dalai Lama to handle local government affairs. By then, the Qing central government had officially established a local theocratic regime presided over by leaders of the Gelug Sect of Tibetan Buddhism. The Qing government proclaimed that the high commissioners sent by the central government to govern Tibet enjoyed equal standing with the Dalai Lam and the Panchen Erdeni.

In 1793 troops sent by the Qing central government repelled an invasion by the Gurkhas (living in today's Nepal). Then the Qing government ordered the commanders of the Qing troops in Tibet and the high commissioners to formulate the 29-article Authorized Regulations for the Better Government of Tibet. These regulations prescribed that the authenticity of the reincarnation of the great Living Buddha is determined by drawing lots from a golden urn, and that the choice must be recognized and appointed by the emperor before he was installed.

The Question of Sovereignty

II

6. When did Tibet come under the administrative jurisdiction of the central government of China? Why do we say Tibet is not an "occupied country" but an inseparable part of China's territory?

Tibet has been an inseparable part of China since ancient times. Since time immemorial the Tibetan people living on the Tibetan Plateau have had close contacts with the Han people in the hinterland and other ethnic groups, all contributing to the founding of a unified multi-ethnic country. In 1247 Sapan, the Tibetan religious leader, and Godan, a Mongolian prince stationed in Liangzhou, reached an agreement on the submission of Tibet. Since then, Tibet has been officially an administrative region under the jurisdiction of the central government.

Throughout the subsequent centuries, the administration by the central government over Tibet was institutionalized and standardized gradually, including the power to take direct charge of setting up local administrative bodies, appoint and dismiss local officials, to check the population and household registrations, and station troops. The central government of the Qing Dynasty set up the post of high commissioners to supervise the management of Tibetan affairs on its behalf. On May 23, 1951 the Agreement Between the Central People's Government and the Local Government of Tibet on Measures for the Peaceful Liberation of Tibet was signed, and Tibet won its peaceful liberation. To this day, no country or international organization has publicly acknowledged that Tibet is an independent country.

7. Is it true that the relationship between China and Tibet has historically been characterized as that between religious offerings and charity, or by that between suzerainty and dependency?

Tibet practiced theocracy for hundreds of years. Throughout the Yuan, Ming and Qing dynasties, the central authorities conferred titles on the religious leaders of various sects in Tibet, and granted power to them to rule Tibet. The local leaders received donation and offerings from and swore fealty to the emperor, accepted conferment of titles and the leadership of the central government, and executed its orders, recognizing Tibet as a subordinate region under the administration of the central government. Since the Yuan Dynasty, the central government has exercised the power to set up local administrative bodies, appoint local officials, send troops, draft labor and check the population and household registries, effectively exercising sovereignty over Tibet.

At the beginning of the 20th century the concept of "suzerainty" was fabricated by the British colonialists. It is meaningless, and can't change the fact that Tibet is part of China.

8. How did the idea of "Tibet independence" come into being? Why do we say that the imperialists and colonialists are behind the "Tibet independence" conspiracy?

Tibet has been an inseparable part of China since ancient times. The central government of China has been exercising sovereignty over Tibet for hundreds of years, and Tibet has never been an independent state. There are several million pieces of documentation written in the Chinese, Tibetan and Manchu languages and historical relics recording historical facts over a thousand years proving this. They are kept in cultural relics departments and archives in Beijing, Nanjing and Lhasa.

The so-called "Tibet independence" is a result of imperialist aggression against China. Until the beginning of 20th century there was no such word as "independence" in the Tibetan language. After the Opium Wars of the 1840s China was reduced to a semi-colonial country, and the imperialists began to take this opportunity to carve up Chinese territory, Tibet included. At the turn of 19th century the United Kingdom launched two invasions of Tibet. As these attempts failed, it began to cultivate pro-British forces in Tibet, and advocate "Tibet independence" to separate Tibet from China. With the strenuous efforts of the Chinese government and people, the scheme for "Tibet independence" failed. Historical facts over the past 100 years explicitly demonstrate that the so-called "Tibet independence" has been cooked up by old and new imperialists out of their craving to wrest Tibet from China.

At present, the separatist clique headed by the 14th Dalai Lama foments "Tibet independence" activities with the support of Western anti-China forces, with the aim of restoring feudal serfdom in Tibet, and sabotaging national unity and territorial integrity.

9. Some people think that Tibet gained de facto independence after the Revolution of 1911. Is this true?

After the Revolution of 1911, incited by the imperialists, the relationship between the local government of Tibet and the central government was abnormal for a period, but the fact that Tibet is part of Chinese territory never changed, and Tibet never gained independence or broke free from the sovereignty of the central government.

After the Revolution of 1911, the Provisional Constitution of the Republic of China, the first Constitution promulgated by the Republic of China, stipulated that Tibet was part of Chinese territory. The Nationalist government then set up a special agency to administer Tibetan affairs. Representatives from the Tibet local government attended many political meetings, including those of the National Assembly, held by the Nationalist government after 1913. The Nationalist government sent officials to attend the memorial service of the 13th Dalai's Parinirvana, approve the reincarnation of the 13th Dalai Lama, and host the installation ceremony of the 14th Dalai Lama. All these indicate that the central government still exercised full sovereignty over Tibet.

Reference:

1. The agencies set up by the Nationalist central government to administer Tibetan affairs included the Office for Mongolian and Tibetan Affairs, Bureau for Mongolian and Tibetan Affairs, Council for Mongolian and Tibetan Affairs, and Commission for Mongolian and Tibetan Affairs.

2. The "soul boy" of the 14th Dalai Lama, now in exile, was approved by the president of the Nationalist government, which sent officials for this purpose in 1940 to Lhasa, at the same time giving consent to the Tibet local government which applied to suspend the practice of drawing lots from a golden urn for the recognition.

3. The Tenth Panchen Lama was approved in June 1949 by the interim president of the Nationalist government.

10. Were the Simla Conference and Simla Accord of the early 20th century legitimate? What is the McMahon Line?

In 1913, seeking to bolster international recognition of Yuan Shikai, who had usurped the position of president of the Republic of China, the British government forced the Yuan Shikai administration to attend a meeting between officials of Britain, China and Tibet in the Indian city of Simla. Prior to the meeting, the British government sent its official resident in Sikkim to Gyantse to meet the delegate of the Tibet local government, Lonchen Shatra Paljor Dorje, in private to incite him to request "Tibet independence," and prevent the high commissioners sent by the Chinese central government from entering Tibet. Incited by Britain, the Tibetan delegates put forward a demand for "Tibet Independence," claiming that Tibet should be independent and include the areas of Qinghai, Litang, Batang and Dajianlu. This was instantly rejected by the delegates of the Chinese central government. At this moment, the British delegate, McMahon, proposed a so-called compromise – to designate regions like part of Xikang which is close to the hinterland, Yunnan and the Tibetan areas of Gansu and Qinghai as Interior Tibet, over which China would exercise sovereignty, and regions like Ü-Tsang, Ngari and the rest of Xikang as Ulterior Tibet, which would have "autonomy." The essence of this scheme was to change China's sovereignty over Tibet into "suzerainty," and separate Tibet from the jurisdiction of the Chinese government. This unreasonable demand immediately met with intense rejection by all the Chinese people, and the delegate of the Chinese government refused to sign the Simla Accord. At the same time, the Chinese government issued a solemn statement refusing to admit such an agreement or document, and notified the British government of its stand. So the Simla Conference broke down, removing the basis for some separatists in exile to preach "Tibet independence" based on the Simla Conference and Simla Accord.

As for the McMahon Line, it was an outgrowth of the Simla Conference of 1914, but was not included on the agenda of that confrerence, which focused on the demarcation line between Tibet and the hinterland, and that between the so-called Interior and Ulterior Tibet. During the Simla Conference, McMahon got certain Tibetan nobles to agree to the McMahon Line, which cut off large areas of Tibetan land and handed them to British India. In return, Britain supported the "Tibet Independence." The Chinese delegates attending the Simla Conference not only refused to sign Simla Accord, but also made a statement at the order of the central government at the conference on July 3, 1914 that the Chinese government refuted all agreements or documents signed between Britain and Tibet on that day or at any other time. This shows that the so-called McMahon Line, marked on the map attached to the Simla Accord, has no legal force. As part of Chinese territory,

Tibet has no power to conclude treaties with foreign governments, and the so-called McMahon Line has no binding force on China. After Simla Conference, as Britain was also aware of the illegitimacy of the McMahon Line, it did not mark this line openly on its maps until 1938, when Japan launched an all-out war of aggression against China, and the Chinese nation was in great dange. It was then that Britain included Simla documents into the revised edition of *Aitchison's Collection of Treaties*, which had been first published in 1929. In 1947, when India gained its independence from Britain, it inherited the expansionist policy promoted by the British colonists, and invaded large areas of Chinese land south of the McMahon Line from 1951 to 1953. The McMahon Line is a product of the policy of aggression by the British colonialists. It has never been recognized by the Chinese government; therefore the Simla Conference, Simla Accord and McMahone Line have no legal force.

11. What was the All-Asia Conference of 1947 about? Did Tibet attend it as an independent state? What is the significance of the snow-lion flag?

At the end of 1946 Britain privately invited the Tibetan local government to attend the All-Asia Conference to be held in New Delhi, India in 1947. The British delegate, Hugh E. Richardson, said that if the local government of Tibet sent a delegate to attend this meeting, it would indicate that Tibet was an independent state. The current situation, he said, made this the perfect moment to push for independence for Tibet. He warned that this should be kept strictly confidential. He then advised the Tibetan delegates to bring a "national flag." The Gaxag, the Tibet local government, decided in a hurry to take a local military flag – the snow-lion flag – as the "national" flag of Tibet. In March 1947 at the All-Asia Conference rigged up by the British imperialists, the snow-lion flag was hung side by side with those of the attending countries, and a map of Asia hung at the conference hall showed Tibet outside Chinese territory, indicating that Tibet was an independent state. After a vigorous protest from the Chinese delegation, India had to rectify the map and remove the snow-lion flag. The All-Asia Conference was an attempt by the imperialists to separate Tibet from Chinese territory. Tibet is part of Chinese territory, and the snow-lion flag is illegal.

12. How was the Agreement Between the Central People's Government and the Local Government of Tibet on Measures for the Peaceful Liberation of Tibet signed? What are its contents?

On October 1, 1949 the Central People's Government of the People's Republic of China was founded in Beijing. Based on the history and actual conditions of Tibet, the central government decided to adopt the policy of peaceful liberation in Tibet, and asked the Tibetan local authorities in January 1950 to send delegates to attend the negotiations on the peaceful liberation of Tibet in Beijing. The 14th Dalai Lama wrote to Chairman Mao, hoping to "receive his concern." In January 1951 the 14th Dalai Lama and Tibet local government accepted the proposal to conduct peace negotiations, and sent a delegation headed by Ngapoi Ngawang Jigme to Beijing to hold talks with the central government. On May 23 the chief representative of the Tibet local government, and other delegates, including Ngapoi Ngawang Jigme, Khemed Sonam Wangdu, Thubten Tendar, Thubten Lekmon, Sampo Tanzin Dondrup and the chief representative of the central government Li Weihan, and delegates Zhang Jingwu, Zhang Guohua and Sun Zhiyuan signed in Beijing the Agreement Between the Central People's Government and the Local Government of Tibet on Measures for the Peaceful Liberation of Tibet, which is also referred to as the 17-Article Agreement. At a subsequent conference held by the Tibet local government, attended by the representatives of the Ganden, Drepung and Sera monasteries, monks and lay officials, a document was adopted and submitted to the 14th Dalai Lama, which said that the 17-Article Agreement was of great benefit to Tibet and should be implemented accordingly. This agreement, they affirmed, reflected the aspirations of all ethnic groups in Tibet, as it represented their fundamental interests.

On October 24, 1951 the 14th Dalai Lama cabled Chairman Mao Zedong as follows: "The Agreement Between the Central People's Government and the Local Government of Tibet on Measures for the Peaceful Liberation of Tibet is supported by the local government, and monks and laymen alike. Under the leadership of Chairman Mao and the Central People's Government, they actively help the garrison troops of the People's Liberation Army (PLA) to consolidate the national defense, drive off the imperialist forces and protect state sovereignty and unity." On May 28, 1951 the Panchen Lama and his Kampus Assembly staff released a statement, announcing that on the matter of the peaceful liberation of Tibet the central government and Tibet local government had reached a satisfactory agreement, and from that time the Tibetan people had got rid of the shackles of imperialism and returned to the bosom of the big family of the motherland. "The agreement," they said, "is in compliance with the interests of all the ethnic groups of China and particularly those of Tibet."

The main contents of the 17-Article Agreement are as follows: The Tibetan people shall unite and drive off imperialist aggressive forces from Tibet. The local government of Tibet shall actively assist the PLA to enter Tibet and consolidate the national defense. The Tibetan people have the right to exercise regional ethnic autonomy under the unified leadership of the Central People's Government. The Central Authorities will not alter the existing political system in Tibet, nor the established status, functions and powers of the Dalai Lama. Officials of various ranks shall hold office as usual. The policy of freedom of religious belief shall be carried out, and the religious beliefs, customs and lifestyle of the Tibetan people will be respected. The Tibetan written and spoken language will be preserved, and the educational system of the Tibetan ethnic group shall be developed step by step, as will Tibetan agriculture, livestock raising, industry and commerce. The local people's livelihood shall be improved. The Central People's Government shall handle all external affairs of the area of Tibet. In matters related to various reforms in Tibet, there will be no compulsion on the part of the Central Authorities. The local government of Tibet should carry out reforms on its own accord, and when the people raise demands for reform, they shall be settled by means of consultation with the leading personnel of Tibet. The established status and powers of the Panchen Erdeni shall be maintained as when the 13th Dalai Lama and the Ninth Panchen Erdeni enjoyed amicable relations with each other. Funds needed by the PLA stationed in Tibet shall be provided by the Central People's Government.

13. What is the truth about the 1959 armed rebellion in Tibet? Was it a "peaceful uprising" by the Tibetan people?

On May 23, 1951 the Central People's Government and Tibet local government signed the Agreement Between the Central People's Government and the Local Government of Tibet on Measures for the Peaceful Liberation of Tibet (the "17-Article Agreement"), opening up prospects for the development of the Tibetan people and winning their support. Based on the 17-Article Agreement, the PLA and the central government staff working in Tibet were to actively promote the patriotic united front in the upper-class circles of Tibet. Pro-imperialist separatists should be educated to change their attitude in a tolerant and patient way. However, some of them kept on colluding with foreign imperialists and anti-China forces to sabotage national peace and unification, opposed and even obstructed the implementation of the 17-Article Agreement. In 1951, when the PLA did not yet settle down and was confronted with food supply difficulties, they took advantage of this to thwart the efforts of the Tibetan upper-class patriots and businessmen to sell food to them, attempting to drive away the PLA and its working staff in Tibet. On February 18, 1952 Sitsap (acting regent) Lukhangwa and Losang Tashi of the Tibet local government asserted at the plenary meeting of the local government that "Tibet is an independent state," opposing the stationing of the PLA garrison in Tibet and the 17-Article Agreement. In late March the same year, they incited the so-called "People's Assembly" to submit a petition to the representative of the central government, claiming that "they would take military action to drive away the PLA." They instigated the "People's Assembly" to cause disturbances and friction, and at the same time sent troops to besiege the residence of the representative of the central government, work committee and banks, and fired shots at the residence of Ngapoi Ngawang Jigme, deputy commander of the Tibet Military Area Command. They sent Tibetan troops to occupy the strategic locations around Lhasa, privately asked the Dapon (officer in command of 500 men) of the Tibetan artillery stationed in Shigatse to stir up a riot in Lhasa. Lukhangwa and Losang Tashi were removed from office for violation of the of 17-Article Agreement.

In May 1955, after attending the NPC together with the 14th Dalai Lama in Beijing, Losang Yeshe, the deputy Yongzin (sutra teacher) of the 14th Dalai Lama and Surkhang Wangchen Gelek, Kalon (cabinet minister), on the pretext of holding Buddhist activities, plotted armed rebellion in Ganzi, Litang in Sichuan Province to obstruct the local democratic reform process. In the meantime, the five key figures of the "People's Assembly," including Ngalek Choze, in the name of greeting the 14th Dalai Lama, went to Ya'nga and Kangding to hold subversive activities, and wrote to the 14th Dalai Lama, overtly opposing the 17-Article Agreement, the establishment of the Preparatory Committee for the Tibet Autonomous Region and demanding "Tibet Independence." Incited by Losang Yeshe and supported by the Tibet pro-imperialist aristocracy, an armed rebellion broke out, first in Kham and then spreading quickly to Qamdo and Lhasa. In 1956, when the 14th Dalai Lama went to India to attend the commemorative activities at the 2,500th anniversary of Shakyamuni, he was soon surrounded by separatists, who tried to force him to lead the "Tibet independence" activities there.

As for the various reforms in Tibet, the central government made specific instructions: The local government of Tibet should carry out reforms on its own accord, and when the people raised demands for reform, they should be settled by means of consultation with the leading personnel of Tibet. There would be no compulsion on the part of the Central Authorities. But implementation of the 17-Article Agreement was not plain sailing, and in 1956, when the Preparatory Committee for the Tibet Autonomous Region was established, some representatives raised the question of the reform of the Tibet social system in accordance with the demand of the local people. Given the actual situation in Tibet in 1957, the central government decided not to carry out democratic reform in Tibet for the next six years, and its implementation after six years would depend on the situation in Tibet at that time. But, aiming to maintain feudal serfdom and the privileges of the feudal lords to oppress and exploit the Tibetan people, some of the reactionary aristocrats in Tibet demanded that its social system should never be changed. Urged and plotted by the upper-class separatists, rebels in Kham, headed by Adruktsang Gonpo Tashi, went to Lhasa and formed an organization called the "Four Rivers and Six Mountain Ranges" in May 1957, and then it rounded up 27 rebellious armed forces and set up the "Four Rivers and Six Mountain Ranges Religion Protecting Army" in July 1958. They opposed any reform, committed such acts as burning, looting, killing, and ran roughshod everywhere. The 14th Dalai Lama made no move to quash the rebellion; instead, he accepted a golden throne they sent to him, and gave them presents in return, demonstrating that he was on the side of the rebellious armed force. In 1959, incited by British and American imperialists aiming to split China by means of promoting the "Tibet independence," this group spread the rumor that the PLA intended to kidnap the 14th Dalai Lama and poison him. On the pretext of protecting the 14th Dalai Lama, they staged an uprising on March 10, and tore up the 17-Article Agreement. On March 17, the 14th Dalai Lama fled Lhasa and emerged as the head of the insurgency, declaring that he had established an "independent Tibet." About 7,000 insurgents launched an all-round attack on the party, government and PLA organs on the morning of March 20. The PLA began a counter-attack at 10 a.m. that morning, and with the support of patriotic

Tibetan monks and lay people, completely put down the armed rebellion with only 1,000 soldiers in Lhasa within two days. On March 28 the Central People's Government abolished the Tibet local government, and established a Preparatory Committee for the Tibet Autonomous Region to function as the local government.

14. What was behind the armed rebellion in Tibet? Who participated in it? What role did foreign forces play?

On May 23, 1951 representatives of the Central People's Government and Tibet local government signed the 17-Article Agreement bestowing peaceful liberation on Tibet. Given the history and the actual conditions of Tibet, the Central People's Government took a very prudent attitude and made tolerant policies concerning reform of the Tibet social system, patiently persuading and waiting for Tibet's ruling elite to carry out the reform on their own initiative. But some of them, in order to safeguard their vested rights and privileges as serf owners, opposed any kind of reform, aiming to maintain the feudal theocracy in perpetuity. They violated the 17-Article Agreement, and even went so far as to incite secessionist activities and even armed rebellion.

In March and April 1952, Sitsap (acting regent) Lukhangwa and Losang Tashi of the Tibet local government implicitly backed the illegal organization known as the "People's Assembly" to make trouble and cause riots in Lhasa, overtly opposing the 17-Article Agreement and demanding that the PLA withdraw from Tibet. In May 1955, when the 14th Dalai Lama returned to Sichuan Province from the hinterland, his companions Losang Yeshe, who was his deputy Yongzin (sutra teacher), and Surkhang Wangchen Gelek, who was the Kalon (cabinet minister) of the Tibet local government, went separately to Tibet via Ganze and Dege in the north and Qacheng and Litang in the south to incite the headmen and abbots en route to oppose the democratic reform with force. Ngalek Choze and the other four leaders of the "People's Assembly" conspired with a secret agent of the Nationalist government at Litang Monastery to raise an armed rebellion. In 1957 Lozang Samten, the third brother of the 14th Dalai Lama, authorized Abbot Chimed Gonpo to follow the "instructions of the 14th Dalai Lama" and launch an insurgency. In May 1957, supported by the Kalons of the Tibet local government, Neushar Thubten Tharpa and Shankha Gyumey Dorije, the "Four Rivers and Six Mountain Ranges" organization openly preached "Tibet independence" and opposed reform. Soon an armed force called "Four Rivers and Six Mountain Ranges Religion Protecting Army" was established. Incited by these reactionaries, an armed rebellion broke out.

The armed rebellion in Tibet had the support of foreign anti-China forces from the very beginning. Western media reported on January 26, 1971 that the intelligence agency of a certain country trained insurgents of the "Four Rivers and Six Mountain Ranges" on an island in the Pacific in February 1957. From 1956 to 1957, that intelligence agency selected 170 insurgents and trained them in the "Kangba Guerrilla Training

Base." They were later parachuted into Tibet, each equipped with a machine gun and wearing a little gold casket containing the 14th Dalai Lama's photograph. This intelligence agency trained 2,000 Tibetan rebels. From July 1958 to February 1959, the agency airdropped weapons twice to the Four Rivers and Six Mountain Ranges Religion Protecting Army, including 403 rifles, 20 light machine guns, 60 boxes of grenades and bags of Indian currency. In November 1958 this intelligence agency transported 226 loads of weaponry to rebel force in Shannan Prefecture via the Indian-occupied area south of the so-called McMahon Line. In January 1959 it supplied 40 loads of goods and materials via Nepal to those rebels. It conducted over 30 airdrops to the rebel forces in Kham, supplying a total of 250 tons of goods and materials, including nearly 10,000 M-1 rifles, submachine guns, 57mm recoilless guns and anti-aircraft guns. According to another report in the Western media on August 16, 1999, from 1957 to 1960 a Western country airdropped over 400 tons of goods and materials to Tibetan guerillas, "spending as many as US$1.7 million in assistance to the Tibet rebellion every year."

As the 14th Dalai Lama fled, that intelligence agency airdropped food, maps, radios, banknotes, etc. along his way, kept in contact with the rebel forces by short-wave radios, and photographed the whole event.

15. What is the Tibetan government-in-exile? Is it a "democratic government"?

After the 14th Dalai Lama escaped India, he first resided at Mussoorie and then moved to Dharamsala, which has been his headquarters ever since. In September 1960 the 14th Dalai Lama and his followers held the first session of the so-called "Tibetan People's Assembly," which announced the setting up of the "Tibetan government-in-exile" and the draft of its constitution. The 14th Dalai Lama was declared "head of state." In 1963 the 14th Dalai Lama clique officially publicized the "Constitution of the State of Tibet," drafted by foreigners, which stipulated that "on the basis of the spirit imparted by the Buddha, Tibet will be a democratic and united country." After revision, it was promulgated again in 1991 as the "Constitution of Tibetans in exile." The so-called Tibetan government-in-exile which is composed of a small group of aristocratic monks and lay reactionaries, former Tibet local government officials, chiefs and headmen from various Tibetan areas, was set up with elaborate plans by imperialists and international anti-China forces. To this day, no country in the world recognizes the so-called Tibetan government-in-exile.

After the 14th Dalai Lama clique fled abroad, it kept up the practice of theocracy. Their so-called constitution stipulates that the 14th Dalai Lama is not only the leader of the Tibetan Buddhist religion, but also the head of state with the right to make final decisions on all major affairs of the government-in-exile. Moreover, the 14th Dalai Lama's brothers and sisters all have important positions in the government-in-exile, controlling the crucial departments. Five Kalons including the Chief Kalon came from his family. The 14th Dalai Lama's family and the other major families have always kept a firm grip on politics, economy, education and the military of the government-in-exile, as well as its funds. Although in recent years they outwardly imitate the West by adopting "democratic elections," and "division of powers," in fact, the final decisions are still made by the 14th Dalai Lama. The politics of the government-in-exile are intensely influenced by religion. No matter how democratic the 14th Dalai Lama clique claims that this government is, in essence still a theocratic ruling agency jointly dominated by senior monks, laymen and aristocrats. In Tibet and other Tibetan areas theocracy has been abolished, democratic reform completed, regional ethnic autonomy with the people as the masters established and socialist political democracy promoted. However, the democracy the 14th Dalai Lama and his international supporters claim are nothing but a sham.

16. Why do Western leaders meet the 14th Dalai Lama? Why does the Chinese government oppose the 14th Dalai Lama's visits to other countries?

In recent years American and some other Western state leaders have officially received the 14th Dalai Lama, and awarded him medals, which are interventions in China's internal affairs, having a negative effect on China's relations with these countries. The 14th Dalai Lama is not just a religious figure, but also a political exile long engaged in trying to split China and sabotaging national unity. No matter what excuses he makes and no matter where he goes, it's not just religious activities or personal business, he represents but a political force aiming to split China and preach the "Tibet Independence." The Chinese government resolutely opposes the 14th Dalai Lama's engaging in such political activities in any form or guise, and opposes political figures of all countries meeting the 14th Dalai Lama on any occasion.

We hope that state leaders and governments will be highly vigilant against the 14th Dalai Lama clique's words and acts aimed at splitting China and damaging the relationship between China and other countries, adopt wise and far-sighted policies, keep their promise not to support the "Tibet independence " or the secessionist activities of the 14th Dalai Lama and his clique, and avoid intervening in China's internal politics when it comes to Tibet issue.

17. What is the role of the "special coordinator for Tibetan affairs" in the United States?

Tibet is an inseparable part of China, and Tibetan affairs are accordingly purely internal affairs of China. The Chinese government does not recognize this so-called "special coordinator for Tibetan affairs" and eschews all ties with it.

Human Rights

18. What social system was practiced in Tibet before the "Democratic Reform"? How was the then human rights situation in Tibet?

Before the Democratic Reform in 1959 Tibet had long been a society of feudal serfdom under the despotic religious-political rule of lamas and nobles, a society which was darker and crueler than European serfdom in the Middle Ages. In this social system ordinary Tibetans, accounting for the majority of the Tibetan population, were merely serfs and slaves deprived of human rights.

The local government of Tibet practicing theocracy was composed of high-ranking lamas and nobles. The Dalai Lama was both the religious leader and the head of the local Tibetan authority. Serfs and slaves, accounting for over 95% of Tibet's total population, didn't possess any means of production. They were deprived of personal freedom and political, economic and cultural rights, and were attached to the three major classes of estate-holders throughout their lives. The estate-holders could punish, sell, give as gift, or even imprison and kill serfs and slaves at will. The serf-owners had a firm grip on the birth, death and marriage of serfs. Male and female serfs had to gain permission from their owners before they married. Children of serfs were registered the moment they were born, setting their life-long fate as serfs. Sons would belong to the husband's owner, and daughters to the wife's owner. Serfs and slaves would announce their owners' names instead of their own at their first meeting. Ancient Tibetan legal codes divided people into three classes and nine ranks, which meant that people were unequal in legal status. The law concerning the penalties for murder stipulated that the lives of people of the highest rank of the upper class, such as nobles and Living Buddhas, were calculated to be literally worth their weight in gold. The lives of people of the lowest rank, such as women, butchers and craftsmen, were worth only a straw rope. Courts and prisons in old Tibet adopted dozens of cruel punishments, such as gouging out the eyes, cutting off the ears, chopping off the hands and feet, pulling out the tendons and drowning.

Under the theocracy of old Tibet, the area was stalled in economic stagnation, with deadly diseases running rampant. The average life expectancy of ordinary Tibetan people was only 35.5, and the illiteracy rate was above 90%. The urban population of Lhasa was more than 20,000 before the Democratic Reform , but this figure included about 1,000 households of paupers and beggars, and the homeless and those who froze or starved to death lined the streets.

Abundant historical materials show that in old Tibet the basic human rights of ordinary Tibetan people were seriously violated. As the then largest serf-owner and head of the theocratic system, the 14th Dalai Lama, who still remains at large, bears an unshakable responsibility for this.

19. Why was the Democratic Reform implemented in Tibet in 1959? What is the significance of "Tibetan Serfs Emancipation Day"?

The 17-Article Agreement explicitly stipulated that reform would be implemented in Tibet, while "In matters relating to various reforms in Tibet, there will be no compulsion on the part of the Central Authorities. The local government of Tibet shall carry out reforms of its own accord, and, when the people raise demands for reform, they shall be settled by means of consultation with the leading personnel of Tibet."

Before the Preparatory Committee for the Tibet Autonomous Region was established in 1956, areas inhabited by Tibetan in the neighboring provinces were also preparing for or about to carry out reforms. The mass of Tibetan people and some open-minded upper-class Tibetans were expecting reforms and advocating changing Tibet's social system as soon as possible. But the majority of the upper-class Tibetans remained doubtful about it, and especially the reactionaries among them were firmly against reform. In view of the actual situation of Tibet, especially considering the upper-class attitude, the central government put forward the principle of "no reform for six years." Some upper-class Tibetans took the central government's patience as weakness, and launched an armed rebellion in 1959.

In this situation the central government, in compliance with the aspirations of the local people, crashed the rebellion and implemented the Democratic Reform. The Democratic Reform abolished the privileges of the "three major estate-holders" accounting for only five percent of Tibet's total population, and emancipated the serfs and slaves, who thus became their own masters. It was an epoch-making reform in Tibetan history as well as significant progress in human rights development.

However, due to the Dalai clique's distorted propaganda spread worldwide, trying to beautify the dark history of old Tibet as a heavenly "Shangri-La," some countries and their people know little about Tibet's history. In the meantime, over 50 years has passed since the 1959 Democratic Reform, some young Tibetan people are not very clear about this history. Therefore, people from all ethnic groups in Tibet requested the establishment of a memorial day to present to their descendants and the world at large the true history of Tibet. On January 19, 2009, in compliance with the will and aspiration of all ethnic groups in Tibet, the Second Session of the Ninth People's Congress of the Tibet Autonomous Region set March 28 as Tibetan Serfs Emancipation Day.

20. What have been the changes in Tibet's human rights situation since the Democratic Reform?

Since the peaceful liberation of Tibet over 50 years ago, the human rights situation in Tibet has been fundamentally improved. Under the care of the central government and with the efforts of the Tibet local governments at all levels, Tibet's human rights situation has been continuously enhanced. Since the peaceful liberation, and especially in the era of the reform and opening-up, the People's Government of the Tibet Autonomous Region put people's rights to subsistence and development in first place, is energetically developing the productive forces and improving the people's living standard, so as to accelerate Tibet's economic development and advance its comprehensive social progress. Now, Tibet's human rights situation is at the highest point in Tibet's history.

Tibetan people enjoy full political rights: Citizens from all ethnic groups in Tibet have the right to vote and to be elected, and manage their own affairs through democratically elected representatives. Since the establishment of the Tibet Autonomous Region in 1965, in each of its people's congresses representatives of the Tibetan and other minority ethnic groups account for an overwhelming proportion. Now Tibet has over 20 deputies to the National People's Congress (NPC), and over 70% of them are from the Tibetan or other minority ethnic groups. The People's Congress of the Tibet Autonomous Region and its Standing Committee have promulgated over 250 regulations, covering politics, economy, culture, education, public health, environment and other fields. The Eighth People's Congress of the Tibet Autonomous Region formulated and revised 35 local regulations, and proposed and reported amendments to 61 national laws.

The Tibetan people's right to subsistence and development has been continuously improved: Since the peaceful liberation of Tibet, the central government has attached great importance to the development of Tibet, and has adopted preferential policies in Tibet while providing massive manpower, material resources and financial support. Tibet has witnessed rapid economic and social development. Transport, energy, communications and other infrastructure construction that are closely connected with the people's daily life have been increasingly enhanced; the urban and rural living environments have been further improved; and the people's living standard has been remarkably elevated. The per capita net income of farmers and herdsmen of the Tibet Autonomous Region in 2009 was 3,532 yuan, and the urban per capita disposable income was 13,544 yuan. Currently, the majority of people living in poverty in the agricultural and pastoral areas have had the problem of food and clothing solved for them, and a small number of them have started to live a well-off life. A transport network focusing on railway and highway construction and facilitated by airline and pipeline development has been formed in Tibet. By the end of 2009 the highway mileage in Tibet had reached 53,845 km, an increase of 2,531 km compared to the previous year, and the total mileage of paved roads had reached 3,279 km, an increase of 384 km. Now 67% of the counties in Tibet have proper asphalt-paved roads, as do 97.95% of the towns and townships, and 80.25% of the large villages. An energy system focusing on hydropower and supplemented by geothermal power, solar power and wind power has been established throughout the region. In 2009 Tibet's total installed electricity capacity reached 720,000 kw, and electricity generation exceeded 1.8 billion kwh, giving 2.1 million people access to electricity. By the end of 2009 some 1.222 million people had been supplied with safe drinking water, and over 85% of Tibet's population is expected to have safe drinking water by 2020. Housing conditions have been dramatically improved. In 2009 the rural per capita housing area was 23.62 sq m, and the urban one was 33.83 sq m. The housing project for farmers and herdsmen started in 2006 will further improve their housing conditions when completed. A satellite ground station with Lhasa as the center and connecting all cities in Tibet has been built. International and domestic long-distance automatic telephone service is available, and most counties are connected to the national automatic long-distance exchange network. By the end of 2009 the telephone switchboard capacity of the autonomous region had reached 419,900 lines, and the number of fixed telephone users had reached 539,300, of whom 512,100 were urban users and 27,200 rural users. All counties are now connected to the Internet; post and telecommunication network is further improved. In the meantime, Tibet has vigorously implemented a sustainable development strategy, and strengthened ecological construction and environmental conservation, with people's right to subsistence and development fully guaranteed.

The Tibetan people have the right to receive education: Except for monastery education and two small schools set up by the Tibet local government for clerical officials and aristocratic children, the old Tibet had no proper schools. The school-age children enrollment rate was less than 2%, and the illiteracy rate of young and middle-aged people was 95%.

To improve the Tibetan people's education level and abilities, the Tibet Autonomous Region People's Government has put special efforts into developing basic education and eliminating illiteracy among young and middle-aged people. Now, the average years of schooling in Tibet have reached 6.3. Besides, literacy classes and night schools are open to illiterate adults, especially to those below 50 years of age, which has reduced the illiteracy rate among young and middle-aged people to less than 2.4%.

In 1959 the first secondary vocational and technical school was opened in the Tibet Autonomous Region. During the Tenth Five-Year Plan period (2001-2005) Tibet began to develop higher vocational and technical education. Now, the number of higher vocational and technical school students in Tibet has exceeded 5,000. Vocational education in Tibet, starting from scratch, has developed rapidly.

With the full support of the central government, vocational training bases are being set up in the Tibet Autonomous Region. Practical technical training for farmers and herdsmen covers crop production, animal husbandry and maintenance of farm machinery. Vocational training is also provided for superfluous labor in farming and pastoral areas.

In addition to improving its own school conditions, Tibet has started to open classes and schools in the hinterland by using the local superior teaching resources. Since 1985 some 18 provinces and cities have provided a total of 576 million yuan for Tibet's education, and renovated over 300 kindergartens, and primary and middle schools in 74 counties in Tibet. Since 1985 the central government has set up Tibetan classes and schools in 20 inland provinces and cities covering all levels of education from junior middle school to university.

While steadily promoting modern education, Tibet attaches special importance to Tibetan-language education. The Constitution of the People's Republic of China and Law of the People's Republic of China on Regional Ethnic Autonomy both explicitly stipulate that the ethnic minorities' freedom to use and develop their own languages is guaranteed. The Regulations of the Tibet

Autonomous Region on the Study, Use and Development of the Tibetan Language, revised in 2002, reinforced the legal status of the Tibetan language in Tibet's educational endeavors.

The total education expenditure of the autonomous region in 2009 was 6.107 billion yuan. In the same year, Tibet's six regular higher education institutions enrolled 9,248 students, including 228 postgraduate students, 9,020 junior college students and graduate students; the number of students in those institutions was 30,853, including 589 postgraduate students, 30,264 junior college students and graduate students; and 8,594 students graduated, including 140 postgraduates and 8,454 graduates. That same year, the six secondary vocational schools enrolled 11,038 students and 3,603 graduated, altogether there were 21,357 students in such schools. Tibet has 118 middle schools, including 15 senior middle schools, nine combined junior and senior high schools, and 94 junior middle schools. The senior middle schools received 13,884 students and 13,312 graduated. There were 38,383 students studying in such schools. The junior middle schools received 50,042 students and 42,401 graduated. There were 143,187 students studying in such schools. The 884 primary schools received 53,682 students and 50,850 graduated. There were 305,235 students learning in such schools. The special schools received 11 students, and altogether there were 200 students studying in such schools. By the end of 2009 a total of 16,068 children were in kindergartens, an increase of 1,401 compared to the previous year. The school-age children enroll-ment rate of the autonomous region reached 98.8%, an increase of 0.3 percentage points over the previous year.

Before the 1959 Democratic Reform Tibet had only three official Tibetan medical institutions and a few poorly equipped private clinics. There were less than 400 medical staff – a rate of 0.4 per 1,000 people. Following the Democratic Reform the central government adopted special health policies for the Ti-bet Autonomous Region, under which individual health savings accounts are supplemented by government subsidies in urban areas, and free medical services are provided in farming and pastoral areas. From 1959 to 2008 the country allocated spe-cial funds totaling over 1.8 billion yuan for the development of Tibet's medical and health work, providing an annual medical subsidy of more than 20 million yuan to the local farmers and herdsmen. By the end of 2008 there were 1,339 medical institu-tions in Tibet, over 20 times the number in 1959; the total num-ber of hospital beds was increased from 480 in 1959 to 7,127 in 2008 – 2.50 beds per 1,000 people in 2008 and 2.11 more than that in 1959. The number of hospital beds and medical staff per 1,000 people in Tibet is higher than the national average and even higher than that of middle-income countries.

Currently, major endemic diseases jeopardizing public health in Tibet have been eliminated or effectively controlled. The iodized salt coverage rate has reached 66%, and the children's immunization rate is above 97%.

In 2009 Tibet's total medical expenditure was 2.184 billion yuan. There were 763 hospitals and health clinics, 81 disease prevention and control centers (health control agencies), 57 maternal and child care service centers, clinics and stations in the autonomous region, providing 5,368 hospital beds among the total of 8,553 ward beds, and 3,395 medical practitioners among the total of 10,047 medical technical staff. The average medical subsidy for farmers and herdsmen was 140 yuan, of which 125 yuan was in the form of a central government financial subsidy and 15 yuan as an autonomous region subsidy.

People in Tibet have the right to cultural inheritance and development. Traditional Tibetan culture is a significant component of the overall Chinese culture; China attaches importance to the conservation, development and prosperity of Tibetan culture. To inherit and promote traditional Tibetan culture, the country has established Tibet University, Tibet University for Nationalities, Tibet Agricultural and Animal Husbandry College, China Tibetology Research Center, Tibet Academy of Social Sciences, and other academically advanced education bases and research institutes with a full range of specialties. They have attracted a large number of outstanding experts and scholars. The old Tibet had no modern Tibetology research at all, but now there is a grand academic system for the comprehensive study of Tibetan society. Now China has more than 60 Tibetology research institutes and over 1,000 experts and scholars specializing in social, economic, cultural, medical, transportation, tourism and other fields. The flourishing of Tibetology will exert a profound influence on the conservation and inheritance of Tibetan society, culture and medicine. In 2006 the national award for Tibetology research – the Qomolangma Award of China Tibetology Research – was instituted.

China attaches great importance to the study, use and development of the Tibetan language, and therefore safeguards the Tibetan ethnic group's freedom to use and develop its own language. Traditional Tibetan medicine is being developed, and has become a pillar industry in the Autonomous Region supported by the local government. Tibet has also carried out wide-ranging and systematic surveys, collecting, recording, compiling, researching on, editing and publishing local folk arts and other aspects of the Tibetan cultural heritage. In recent years the autonomous region has published dozens of books and journals in the Tibetan language annually, with a total circulation of over 100,000. Tibetan terminology and information technology standardization of the Tibetan language have achieved significant progress. Encoding of the Tibetan language has reached national and international standards. The Tibetan language has become China's first ethnic-minority language with an international standard.

In 2009 the radio and television coverage rate in Tibet had reached 89.2% and 90.36%, respectively. It has long been the goal of the autonomous region's government to provide the local farmers and herdsmen with more and better-quality films. In 2009 Tibet vigorously promoted the digitization process of film projection and increased the availability of outdoor movie venues, strengthened rural digital cinema construction, and advocated diversified rural cinema ownership and subsidies for film production.

Digital cable TV has been first made available to government organs of the Autonomous Region and the city of Lhasa. Construction of digital cable TV has been accelerated in prefecture-level cities, with a number of areas' projects already completed. At present, Tibet has one regional broadcasting station, one regional TV station, three prefectual-level radio-TV stations and four TV stations.

Tibet now has 44 art troupes at various levels, including the Tibet Autonomous Region Song and Dance Troupe, Modern Drama Troupe and Lhasa Ballad Troupe, as well as other flourishing arts organizations. There are four libraries, 208 community culture centers, 17 cultural relics institutions and 86 publishing institutions. These bodies have a total of 1,828 staff members. The Tibetan people now enjoy the full right to cultural innovation and appreciation.

People in the Tibet Autonomous Region enjoy full freedom of religious belief. The Chinese government constantly respects and protects the people's freedom of religious belief, and has a special stipulation about it in the Constitution of the People's Republic of China, Law of the People's Republic of China on Regional Ethnic Autonomy and other laws. The Central People's Government has listed the Potala Palace, Jokhang Monastery, Tashilhunpo Monastery, Drepung Monastery, Sera Monastery, Sakya Monastery, and other noted religious venues in Tibet as key cultural relics sites under the state's or the autonomous region's protection, and allocated special funds, gold and silver for the renovation and conservation of these temples. The three renovation projects that started in 2002, namely, those of the Potala Palace, Norbulingka and Sakya Monastery, have received state funds totaling 300 million yuan. Now Tibet has a total of 1,780 religious venues, over 46,000 monks and nuns practicing their faith in such venues, and 358 Living Buddhas, 46 of whom were approved by governments at various levels in accordance with the Reincarnation System of Living Buddhas. In addition, some people in Tibet believe in Islam or Catholicism. Various religious activities are held in an orderly manner, with people's religious demands completely fulfilled and their freedom of religious belief fully respected.

The seven prefecture-level cities in Tibet all have set up Buddhist associations. The Tibet Branch of the Buddhist Association of China issues a Buddhist journal, *Tibet Buddhism*, and runs printing houses for Buddhist texts in the Tibetan language.

21. Since the Democratic Reform in 1959, how has Tibet's population changed? The 14th Dalai Lama has repeatedly claimed that China has eliminated 1.2 million Tibetans, is this true?

In 1953 China launched its first national census. This was not long after Tibet's peaceful liberation, and the original Tibet local government hadn't conducted any census. It was estimated at that time that Tibet's population was 1.27 million, which was later found to be 1.1409 million. Therefore, the Dalai Lama's statement is entirely groundless.

In the half-century since the Democratic Reform, Tibet has witnessed remarkable economic and social development, with increasingly improved living standards, better medical and health services, and rapid population growth. By the end of 2009 the permanent population in Tibet was 2.9003 million, 95% of whom were Tibetans and people of other local minority ethnic groups.

22. Does China implement the birth control policy in Tibet? Are there any special policies for Tibet? It is said that there are forced abortions in Tibet; is this true?

China is a large country, with a population of over 1.3 billion. In view of this fundamental reality and to ensure a population growth compatible with social and economic development, the Chinese government promotes the family planning in the principle of government guidance combined with the people's wishes, and has set the control of population growth and improving of population quality as a fundamental national policy. Considering the socio-economic situation of China's ethnic-minority populations, the Chinese government has adopted special policies for them, including the Tibetan ethnic group. It is explicitly stipulated that family planning should also be advocated in ethnic-minority areas, but it should be implemented by the autonomous governments according to local conditions.

Since the birth control policy was implemented nationwide in the early 1970s, the Chinese government has adopted special policies for family planning among the Tibetans. The "one couple, one child" policy is implemented only for Han cadres and employees of state-owned enterprises in Tibet, but not for those of the Tibetan ethnic group. In spite of the large land area of Tibet, its accessible land resources are very limited. In 1991 Tibet's per capita farmland area was only 1.54 *mu*, in spite of the rapid population growth, hence the necessity of population growth control. In 1985 the Tibet Autonomous Region People's Government proposed to adopt family planning in view of the actual situation of Tibet's population development, advocating family planning among cadres and employees of state-owned enterprises of the Tibetan ethnic group, and encouraging each couple to have a second child a few years after they have given birth to the first one. As for farmers and herdsmen, accounting for 77.4 % of Tibet's total population, the government has neither adopted family planning nor ordered a childbirth limit, but advocates scientific contraception with healthy pregnancy, scientific nurture and better maternity and child care instead. As for the sparsely populated border areas in Tibet, the government has not even conducted publicity and education on family planning.

During the implementation of family planning in the Tibet Autonomous Region, the government prohibits forced abortions in any form. How to control population growth in a rational and planned way according to its ecological situation is a practical issue that Tibet has to face in its future socio-economic development.

From the seventh to the 18th century, because of natural disasters, epidemic diseases and poor medical care, and the large number of monks and nuns, Tibet's population was in constant and even rapid decline. During the 200 years from the 18th century to the mid-20th century, Tibet's population was reduced to about 800,000 under the brutal oppression of the feudal serf system.

Since the peaceful liberation of Tibet in 1951 Tibet's population, especially that of the Tibetan ethnic group, has seen its most rapid increase in history. Since 1956 Tibet's birthrate and natural population growth rate have been higher than the national average. By the end of 2009 the permanent population of Tibet was 2.9003 million, an increase of 1.7594 million over that of 1951. The birth control policy widely adopted in China's inland is not implemented in the agricultural and pastoral areas in Tibet. According to a survey conducted by a statistic department among 1% of resident population in Tibet, the annual population growth rate in the past ten years has been above 10‰, much higher than the national average.

Since the introduction of China's reform and opening-up policies, human resources exchanges between Tibet and the hinterland have been invigorated, and a large number of people from other parts of China have moved into Tibet. However, the rapid population growth in Tibet is mainly attributable to the population growth of the local Tibetans. The population of the Tibetans and local residents of other ethnic minorities has long accounted for an overwhelming proportion of the autonomous region's total population, above 95% to be exact, while that of the Tibetan ethnic group alone maintaining a steady 90% or more.

23. In Tibet is anyone arrested for participating in peaceful demonstrations and petition activities? Is anyone arrested for demanding "Tibet independence" or supporting the Dalai Lama?

Article 35 of the Constitution of the People's Republic of China stipulates that citizens of the People's Republic of China enjoy freedom of speech, the press, assembly, association, procession and demonstration. China's Constitution also stipulates that every citizen is entitled to the rights and at the same time must perform the duties prescribed by the Constitution and the law. Citizens of the People's Republic of China, in exercising their freedoms and rights, may not infringe upon the interests of the state, society or the collective, or upon the lawful freedoms and rights of other citizens.

According to Article 13 of the Criminal Law of the People's Republic of China, all acts that endanger the security of the state, subvert the political power of the people's democratic dictatorship and undermine the socialist system are crimes. A small number of people in Tibet, who try to subvert the socialist system, sabotage the unification of the country, undermine ethnic unity, and commit violent crimes should be subject to legal sanctions, so it is not a question of "infringing upon human rights" at all.

24. How is the situation in the prisons in Tibet? Can the prisoners' human rights be guaranteed?

China's Constitution and laws explicitly stipulate that state organs and functionaries should act in accordance with the law and protect the lawful rights and interests of the citizens. The Prisons Law of the People's Republic of China stipulates that the human dignity, personal safety, lawful properties, and rights to defense, petition, complaint and accusation as well as other rights which have not been removed or restricted by law shall not be violated. The Law also prohibits corporal punishment and other forms of maltreatment of prisoners. Prisoners enjoy the right to petition, correspondence and visits, and the rights to receive education, rest, remuneration, labor protection and insurance, and medical and health care. They also enjoy equal rights with other citizens after serving their sentence. To safeguard the lawful rights of prisoners, the Prison Law prescribes strict and specific demands for the staff of prisons: If prisoners' lawful rights are violated, and the case does not constitute a crime, the offenders shall be given administrative sanctions; if the case constitutes a crime, the offenders shall be investigated for criminal liability. Prisons and their staff in Tibet have strictly abided by those laws and regulations, and protected human rights of the prisoners according to law.

25. How can we evaluate the references to Tibet in the US *Human Rights Report*?

China believes that, concerning the issue of human rights, all countries have the right, considering their own development level, with the right to subsistence guaranteed, and upholding the principle of equality and mutual respect, to carry out active dialogue and cooperation to promote better understanding of each other, to seek common ground while shelving differences, and to settle disputes appropriately. The central government has made great efforts to improve the human rights situation in Tibet, which have proved to be fruitful. The achievements are clear for all to see, and cannot be erased simply by a so-called *Human Rights Report*.

26. How are the relations between ethnic groups in Tibet? Is the Tibetan ethnic group harassed by "Han chauvinism"?

Since the founding of the People's Republic of China in 1949, equality, unity, mutual assistance and mutual prosperity among all ethnic groups have become the main trend of China's ethnic relations. Under the guidance of the state and with the support of all other ethnic groups, Tibet has realized regional ethnic autonomy through peaceful liberation and Democratic Reform. The Tibetan people, as a member of the Chinese family, have gained the right to equal participation in state affairs, the right to the autonomy of Tibet and the right to determination of their own fate.

With the rapid development of Tibet's economy and the increasing market opening, the number of migrant workers and businessmen in Tibet is increasing. This floating population composed of both Han people and other ethnic minorities is not large. In the meantime, there are also a number of Tibetans working or doing business in the hinterland, which is a normal population flow in a market economy.

Tibetans and local residents of other ethnic minorities account for 95% of Tibet's total population. Over 40 ethnic groups are living together in Tibet. Under the guidance of sound ethnic policies, all ethnic groups in Tibet have established favorable relations based on equality and unity, mutual care and mutual assistance, relying on each other while striving for common prosperity. Since the March 14 Incident, people from all ethnic groups in Tibet have a deeper understanding of "unity and stability are fortune, split and riots are misfortune," thus strengthening their confidence and determination to safeguard national unification and ethnic unity while opposing efforts to split the country.

Therefore, unequal ethnic relations or Han chauvinism do not exist in Tibet.

27. What policies has the Chinese government adopted toward overseas Tibetans? Does China restrict the access of overseas Tibetans to Tibet?

The Chinese government pays constant attention to the situation of Tibetans living abroad, and has made the principle clear that "all patriots belong to one big family, whether they practice patriotism now or later," so as to achieve the country's great unity based on patriotism. As long as those with separatist behavior stop their activities aimed at splitting the country, they will be welcomed by the motherland and the people. The Chinese government hopes the overseas Tibetans will abide by the laws of their host countries and live in harmony with the local people, while keeping the motherland in mind and contributing to China's unification and ethnic unity.

Patriotic overseas Tibetans are welcome to come back to Tibet and other Tibetan areas to visit family and friends, as pilgrims, tourists or investors, and to make more contributions to the development of their hometowns in accordance with the principle of voluntariness and lawfulness. In recent years, over 1,000 overseas Tibetans have come back to China annually to visit family and friends with travel permits issued by Chinese embassies. However, it is absolutely prohibited for separatists to take advantage of this opportunity to try to split the country, conspire to incite riots and conduct criminal activities in Tibet.

China is a country ruled by law. The Law of the People's Republic of China on the Control of the Exit and Entry of Citizens and the Passport Law of the People's Republic of China have detailed stipulations that protect the exit and entry of citizens with legitimate identity documents and reason for visiting. Illegal immigration, as a violation of law, is forbidden in all countries.

Regional Ethnic
Autonomy

IV

28. What's the basic policy implemented by the central government in Tibet? And why?

China is a unified multi-ethnic country. Regional ethnic autonomy is one of its basic political systems, enshrined in the Constitution, which aims to safeguard national unity, promote equality, solidarity, common development and prosperity among all ethnic groups. As one of the five regions at the provincial level which practice regional ethnic autonomy, the Tibet Autonomous Region enjoys all the rights and obligations specified in the Constitution and relevant laws, and the other national ethnic policies. In the meantime, the state has also introduced measures different from those in other ethnic minority areas, given the peculiarities of the Tibetan region.

On May 23, 1951 the Central People's Government and the local government of Tibet signed the 17-Article Agreement, which stipulated that regional ethnic autonomy was instituted in Tibet. In September 1965 the Tibet Autonomous Region was founded, and the system of regional ethnic autonomy began to be implemented in an all-round way in Tibet.

Reference:

The national policies regarding ethnic minorities are mainly: 1. policy of ethnic equality and unity; 2. policy of regional ethnic autonomy; 3. policy of vigorous training and employment of ethnic minority cadres; 4. policy of accelerating the economic and social development of ethnic minorities and in ethnic minority regions; 5. policy of actively developing and promoting the cultural undertakings of ethnic minorities; 6. policy of actively developing the educational undertakings of ethnic minorities; 7. policy of protecting the rights of ethnic minorities to use and develop their spoken and written languages; 8. policy of respecting the customs and lifestyle of ethnic minorities; 9. policy of respecting the religious freedom of ethnic minorities; 10. policy of establishing a united front with the upper class compatriots of ethnic minorities.

29. What rights are provided by the system of region-al ethnic autonomy to ethnic minorities?

Since the launch of the Democratic Reform in Tibet in 1959 the Tibetans have become the masters of their region and society, like all other ethnic groups, endowed with all the rights empowered by the Constitution and laws. In accordance with the Constitution and the Law of the People's Republic of China on Regional Ethnic Autonomy, the Tibet Autonomous Region enjoys extensive rights of autonomy, which include legislative power, implementation of laws with certain specific alterations, right to use and develop their spoken and written languages, right to manage its personnel and finances, and right to develop its cultural and educational undertakings on its own initiative. Since the establishment of the Tibet Autonomous Region in 1965, the regional people's congress and its standing committee of the Tibet Autonomous Region have formulated over 250 local regulations, resolutions and decisions with legal effect, and enacted implementing measures for a variety of national laws so as to make them more applicable to the conditions of Tibet. In the meantime, a contingent of ethnic minority cadres mainly composed of Tibetans has been formed in the Tibet Autonomous Region, and among the staff of government offices at autonomous region, prefecture (city) and county levels, 77.97% are Tibetans and residents of other ethnic minorities. The practice of regional ethnic autonomy provides a reliable guarantee for the rights of the Tibetan people in the political, economic and cultural aspects.

Reference:

1. The organ of self-government in Tibet has designated the Tibetan New Year, the Shonton Festival and other traditional Tibetan festivals as statutory public holidays in the region, apart from the national public holidays.

2. Out of consideration for the special natural and geographical factors of Tibet, the Tibet Autonomous Region has fixed the work week at 35 hours, five hours fewer than the national statutory work week.

3. It attaches equal importance to the Tibetan and Chinese languages, but gives priority to the Tibetan language. The regulations and decrees of the Tibet Autonomous Region, the official documents and notices issued by governments at all levels in Tibet are all written in both languages. In lawsuits, a court must use the Tibetan language to hear the case if one party involved is Tibetan.

4. The chairperson of the Standing Committee of the People's Congress, and the governor of Tibet Autonomous Region must be Tibetan citizens. Leading positions are mostly assumed by Tibetans and people of other ethnic minorities.

30. Why can't Tibet implement "one country, two systems" like Hong Kong and Macau?

"One country, two systems" is the policy adopted by the central government to solve the issues of Taiwan, Hong Kong and Macau, and to realize the reunification of our country. But the Tibet issue is totally different from those of Taiwan, Hong Kong and Macau. As a result of imperialist invasions, the issues of Hong Kong and Macau were about the resumption of sovereignty. Tibet has been an inseparable part of China's territory since ancient times, over which the central government has always exercised effective sovereign jurisdiction. So the issue of resuming the exercise of sovereignty does not exist.

Democratic Reform in Tibet abolished the feudal serfdom under a theocracy and emancipated millions of serfs. In 1965 the Tibet Autonomous Region was set up, enjoying a variety of autonomy rights prescribed by the Constitution and law, and the Tibetan people's rights to participate in state and local affairs are fully guaranteed. With over 50 years of socialist construction, Tibet's economy is developed, social harmony realized, ethnic unity maintained and the people's peaceful life ensured. Practice demonstrates that the policy of regional ethnic autonomy fits well with the conditions of Tibet, and it has won the full support of Tibetan people.

31. Can the political and legal status of Tibet be decided by referendum?

Tibet has been an inseparable part of China since ancient times, and as an administrative region under the jurisdiction of the central government, its political and legal status is explicit, and its future is not susceptible to a referendum. In recent years, the Dalai Lama asked to solve the "Tibet issue" through a referendum, aiming to manufacture public opinion, extend his influence and gain foreign support to internationalize the "Tibet issue." This is, in essence, an attempt to promote "Tibet independence," and incite secessionist sentiment.

32. How do the people's congresses in the Tibet Autonomous Region function? How are the deputies to the local people's congresses and the NPC, respectively, elected? Who are the Tibetan deputies to the NPC?

In accordance with the Constitution and electoral law, the deputies to the people's congresses at all levels are democratically elected. The deputies to the NPC and the people's congresses of the provinces, autonomous regions, municipalities, cities divided into districts and prefecture are elected indirectly, i.e., through the people's congress at the next lower level.

The number of deputies to the NPC in the Tibet Autonomous Region is arranged by the Standing Committee of the NPC in accordance with the electoral law. The candidates are nominated by the electoral units. All parties, mass organizations and deputies to local people's congresses may recommend candidates to be national deputies jointly or independently, voters, or over ten deputies to local people's congresses may also recommend candidates, who are finally elected by the people's congress of the Tibet Autonomous Region.

The number of deputies to the people's congress of the Tibet Autonomous Region is decided by the Standing Committee of the NPC. The candidates are nominated by constituency or electoral unit, and elected by the people's congresses of Lhasa and the various counties.

There are now 20 deputies from the Tibet Autonomous Region to the NPC, among whom 13 are Tibetans, one is of the Moinba ethnic group, one is of the Lhoba ethnic group, and five are of the Han ethnic group.

33. How do grassroots democratic elections operate in Tibet?

The Organic Law of the Local People's Congresses and Local People's Governments of the People's Republic of China stipulates that the people's congresses at the county and township level exercise the power of electing the heads and deputy heads of counties and townships. The Tibet Autonomous Region holds general elections to the people's congresses at the township and town levels in strict accordance with the law, and elects heads of townships and towns in accordance with statutory procedures and laws.

34. What about the Party's leadership over the people's congresses?

Formed over a long period of time, the CPC's leadership position is explicitly specified in the Constitution. The CPC's leadership of state affairs is manifested in defining political principles, political direction, major decisions and selection of important cadres to state organs. All decisions that should be made by the NPC or its Standing Committee are decided by the NPC or its Standing Committee according to law. As the ruling party, the CPC guides and supports the people in exercising their rights as the masters of the country, and it will not exercise its power on behalf of the NPC and its Standing Committee. The Party's policies are changed into the state will only after being ratified by the NPC in accordance with legal procedures.

The CPC rallies people of all ethnic groups, and CPC members, regardless of their ethnic group, may be appointed as leading cadres of the Party so long as they live up to the regulations of the Party Constitution.

35. What is the situation of socialist democracy and legal system in Tibet?

Before the Democratic Reform of 1959 the serfs and slaves, who made up over 95% of the total population, were deprived of liberty and political rights. The Democratic Reform abolished the theocracy which kept the Tibetan people in feudal serfdom, and made the Tibetan people the masters of the state and society like other ethnic groups, obtaining all the citizens' political rights prescribed by the Constitution and law.

On September 19, 1961 the first Electoral Regulations of the People's Congress of the Tibet Autonomous Region (draft) in the history of Tibet was adopted and promulgated by the Standing Committee of the Preparatory Committee of the Tibet Autonomous Region. It provides that all citizens in the Tibet Autonomous Region who have reached the age of 18 have the right to vote and stand for election, regardless of ethnic status, race, sex, occupation, family background, religious belief, education, property or length of residence. Among the local deputies to the people's congresses at the different levels, those of Tibetan origin and of other ethnicities make up over 80%. The deputies exercise power to manage state and local affairs through people's congresses at various levels. People of all strata and all walks of life in Tibet also exercise their democratic rights by participating in the deliberation and administration of state affairs through the Chinese People's Political Consultative Conference at various levels.

A judicial contingent mostly composed of people of the Tibetan and other ethnic minorities has been established in the Tibet Autonomous Region. The chief officials of the judicial departments at all levels of the Tibet Autonomous Region are appointed and removed by the people's congress at the next-higher level. They should protect the basic rights, freedom, and lawful rights and interests of citizens of all ethnic groups in accordance with the Constitution, laws and regulations, subject to the supervision of the people's congresses at various levels.

36. How do Tibetan officials exercise their rights to manage state and local affairs in the Tibet Autonomous Region?

In accordance with the Constitution and the Law on Regional Ethnic Autonomy, the self-government organs of the Tibet Autonomous Region have the right to formulate and implement local regulations and enjoy autonomy rights which cover all aspects of politics, economy, culture and social life. They include:

1) The right to formulate regulations on the exercise of autonomy and separate regulations in accordance with the local political, economic and cultural conditions, which will take effect after being ratified by the Standing Committee of the NPC;

2) The right to implement state laws and policies, resolutions, decisions, orders and directives of state organs at the next-higher level in accordance with the local conditions. If any of the same is deemed not suitable for the actual situation of the region, the self-government organs of Tibet may flexibly implement or not implement them, upon approval by higher authorities;

3) The right, within the framework of the Constitution and laws, to adopt special policies and flexible measures in accordance with the local conditions to speed up eco-

nomic and cultural development;

4) The freedom to use and develop the local spoken and written languages in performing their duties;

5) The right to train a large number of minority cadres, professionals and technical personnel based on the needs of socialist construction;

6) The right to establish public security force to maintain public order with the authorization of the State Council in accordance with the needs of the state military system and local conditions.

7) The right to manage local finances and arrange local economic development;

8) The right to independently manage local educational, scientific, cultural, health and physical education undertakings, protect and classify local cultural relics, and develop and promote the local culture.

In terms of the building of political power, the Tibet Autonomous Region explicitly stipulates that the proportion of deputies of Tibetan and other ethnic minorities to the local people's congresses at all levels should be no less than 80%. A large number of local residents of Tibet and other ethnic minorities take up leading positions at different levels. Tibetan cadres are the backbone of all undertakings in Tibet, taking charge of the people's congresses, governments and Chinese People's Political Consultative Conference organs at all levels. China is a united multi-ethnic country, and in dealing with matters of national importance, Tibetans and other ethnic minorities have their representatives in the NPC, the highest organ of state power.

The Constitution stipulates that among the chairman and vice chairmen of the standing committee of the people's congress of an ethnic autonomous area there shall be one or more citizens of the ethnic group or groups exercising regional autonomy in the area concerned; the chairman of an autonomous region, the prefect of an autonomous prefecture or the head of an autonomous county shall be a member of the ethnic group exercising regional autonomy in the area concerned. There are citizens of the Tibetan ethnic group and other ethnic minorities participating directly in the management of state affairs, and some hold senior positions in state organs.

Development of Economy and Society

V

37. What has Chinese central government done to develop Tibet's economy? What is China's financial input into this region? Does Tibet enjoy any preferential policies for greater economic and social progress?

Tibet initiated its modernization drive in a state of extreme backwardness as a result of centuries of feudal serfdom. In view of special conditions in Tibet, the central government supports Tibet's development by providing preferential policies, projects and funds, and urges relatively developed provinces and big enterprises to help the region. China's strategy to support Tibet with all-out efforts exemplified the advantages of socialism.

China has held five Tibet Work Symposiums since 1980 to discuss Tibet's development. The Fourth Tibet Work Symposium, held in June 2001, decided to further increase financial input into Tibet and formulate more preferential policies for the region. The meeting decided to intensify the aid from partner provinces and enterprises to Tibet, and extend the term from ten years to 20 years. The central government would also provide a total of 37 billion yuan as financial aid to Tibet during the 10th Five-Year Plan period (2001-2006). The meeting also earmarked for Tibet 117 construction projects involving a total investment of 31.2 billion yuan from the central government, and 70 construction projects involving a total investment of 1.06 billion yuan from various provinces and municipalities. The meeting assigned three additional provinces and 17 state-owned enterprises to assist Tibet's economic development, so that the assistance could cover all of the region's cities and 74 counties and districts. The central government set no limit to the number of projects in Tibet. The government would approve all feasible projects and provide additional projects if needed.

Investment has had a remarkable influence on the economic growth of Tibet. Fixed assets investment in the region soared from 29 million yuan in 1959 to 37.942 billion yuan in 2009 – an annual growth rate of 15.2%. In 1985, the second year of Tibet's adoption of opening-up policy, the investment in fixed assets accounted for 42.2% of that year's GDP, at least ten percentage points more than in the past. From then on, Tibet's investment in fixed assets has grown by a big margin, and the proportion of this in the region's GDP has remained at a relatively high level. In each of the ten years from 1984 to 1994 the proportion of Tibet's investment in fixed assets in its GDP was more than 40%. This figure rose to 66% in 1995, and dropped to between 45% and 47% from 1996 to 1998. After that, Tibet again accelerated its investment in fixed assets. In the six years from 2003 to 2009 the proportion of Tibet's investment in fixed assets in its GDP was more than 75%, over 20 percentage points higher than the national average.

Since Tibet's Democratic Reform in 1959, and especially since China's reform and opening up started in 1978, Tibet has witnessed remarkable economic development. Nonetheless, for various reasons, many challenges remain, including the high cost for economic and social development, underdeveloped market, unbalanced economic and social development in urban and rural areas, low market competitiveness of farmers and herdsmen, and underdeveloped human capital. These are the long-term challenges Tibet has to address in order to achieve sound economic development.

Since Tibet's peaceful liberation in 1951, and especially since China's reform and opening up started in 1978, the central government and the government of the Tibet Autonomous Region have greatly promoted the region's economic development and the living standard of farmers and herdsmen by adopting preferential policies to rehabilitate the farming and pastoral areas. The government has also made preferential policies for Tibet's farmers and herdsmen. In farming areas, "land should be used by individual farm households for their own production, a policy which will be kept unchanged for a long time to come;" in pastoral areas, "livestock should be owned and raised by individual herder households, a policy which will be kept unchanged for a long time to come." The government has exempted township enterprises from income tax, to encourage their development. Farming and animal husbandry are also tax-free. The government provides financial subsidies for purchasing the means of agricultural production, and purchases grain and edible oil from farmers and herdsmen at preferential prices. Farmers and herdsmen receive free medical treatment, and their children enjoy the "three guarantees" (free food, board and tuition fees) for compulsory education. In 2005, the People's Government of Tibet provided allowances to farmers and herdsmen if their annual net income was below 300 yuan. Since 2006 a system of minimum subsistence allowances for rural residents has been instituted across Tibet, and the poverty line for allowances has increased by a big margin to cover families with an average annual per capita income of less than 800 yuan. A total of 230,000 rural families have benefited from the policy. Since 2003 the regional government has several times raised the allowance for elderly people living on their own, the disabled who have lost the ability to work and minors with no source of income. The annual allowance per person has been raised from 588 yuan in the past to 1,600 yuan. In 2009 the regional government again adjusted the poverty line for minimum subsistence allowances, raising the minimum annual per capita income from 850 yuan to 1,100 yuan for rural people, and from monthly 260 yuan to 310 yuan for urban people.

Today most Tibetan people, guaranteed enough food and

clothing, are leading relatively comfortable lives and are heading for a moderately well-off lives.

In 2009 the annual per capita net income of farmers and herdsmen reached 3,532 yuan, more than doubling the figure of 1,331 yuan in 2000.

38. What are the priorities for Tibet in the strategy for the development of the western regions?

The strategy for the development of the western regions is a strategic measure taken by the central government to assist the economic development of the western provinces. The priorities for Tibet are:

1) Accelerating the infrastructure construction, such as transportation, water conservancy, energy and telecommunications to further ease the bottleneck effect of poor infrastructure on economic development.

2) Protecting and improving the ecological environment, and enhancing environmental sustainability and harmony between man and nature.

3) Improving infrastructure related to agriculture and animal husbandry, and in farming and pastoral areas, and improving the living standard of farmers and herdsmen more rapidly.

4) Optimizing the industrial structure, and putting emphasis on industries with regional features and advantageous industries.

5) Accelerating the development of social undertakings such as science, education, public health and culture, so as to achieve all-round social and economic development.

6) Deepening reform and opening up, and facilitating domestic and international exchanges in the fields of economy and technology.

7) Accelerating fostering of talented people in order to provide sufficient talents to implement the strategy for the development of the western regions.

39. How many Tibet Work Symposiums has the central government held? What are the main themes of these symposiums?

The central government, always concerned with the development of Tibet, has held five Tibet Work Symposiums in 1980, 1984, 1994, 2001 and 2010, respectively.

The First Tibet Work Symposium, held in 1980, mainly implemented the lines, principles and policies that had been formulated since the Third Plenary Session of the Eleventh CPC Central Committee in late 1978. The meeting adhered to the ideological line of seeking truth from facts advocated by Deng Xiaoping. It also pointed out that the development of Tibet should rely on the Party, the government and the army organizations, as well as all ethnic groups in Tibet. Various departments of the central government were also asked to provide proper guidance for the work, and mobilize the entire country to help the region. The First Tibet Work Symposium set things right in Tibet after the "cultural revolution (1966-1976)," and shifted the focus of government work from class struggle to economic development.

The Second Tibet Work Symposium, held in 1984, exemplified Deng Xiaoping's thought of emancipating the mind and developing the economy as well as reform and opening up. The meeting decided to further emancipate the mind, act bravely, make full use of Tibet's advantages, and formulate principles and policies in accordance with the actual conditions in Tibet. The meeting decided to adopt the production and management policy centered on family production and market regulation, and turn Tibet from an isolated economy into an open one. The meeting also adopted the household management responsibility system and the two policies that "would be kept unchanged for a long time" – land should be used by individual farm households for their own production, and livestock should be owned and raised by individual herder households. The Second Tibet Work Symposium stimulated Tibet's rapid economic development. Tibet started to turn from being an isolated economy to being an open one.

In 1994 President Jiang Zemin presided over the Third Tibet Work Symposium to implement the spirit of Deng Xiaoping's remarks on his inspection tour of south China. The meeting summed up the historical experience of the work in Tibet from the whole region's strategic point of view, formulated a package of policies to maintain social stability and accelerate economic development. The meeting designated inland provinces to provide coordinated assistance to certain parts of Tibet, setting off a new wave across China of helping Tibet. The meeting, as an important social and economic milestone, also determined 62 assistance projects funded by various inland provinces and departments of the central government, developed agriculture, animal husbandry and infrastructure such as transportation, energy and telecommunications.

President Jiang Zemin presided over the Fourth Tibet Work Symposium from June 25 to 27, 2001. This important meeting was held by the Party Central Committee and the State Council at the beginning of the 21st century and the 50th anniversary of Tibet's peaceful liberation. The meeting, as another important social and economic milestone, defined the guiding principles and the main tasks of the work in Tibet in the new century, and put forward the goal for Tibet to achieve leapfrog development on the basis of accelerated development, and reach lasting stability on the basis of overall stability.

The Party Central Committee and the State Council held the Fifth Tibet Work Symposium in Beijing from January 18 to 20, 2010. The meeting formulated strategic arrangements to promote Tibet's leapfrog development and lasting stability, and accelerated the economic and social development of the Tibetan-inhabited areas in Sichuan, Yunnan, Gansu and Qinghai. The Fifth Tibet Work Symposium was an important meeting held at the critical point of building a well-off society in an all-round way, entering Tibet's leapfrog development stage and fighting separatism. It was an important meeting to ensure Tibet's success in building a well-off society and addressing the people's livelihood issues. The meeting planned for the future, consolidated Tibet's foundation, took the road of development with Chinese and Tibetan characteristics, and embodied the concern of the Party Central Committee headed by President Hu Jintao for the Tibetan people, and the support of the Party, the army, the entire country and people of all ethnic groups for Tibet's development.

40. How will the Fifth Tibet Work Symposium affect the social and economic development of Tibet? What is Tibet's strategy for economic development? What are the key points of the strategy?

The Fifth Tibet Work Symposium was an important meeting held at the critical point of building a well-off society and reaching Tibet's leapfrog development. The meeting made strategic arrangements to promote Tibet's leapfrog development and lasting stability, and clarified the guiding principles, development strategies, tasks, policies and measures for the work in Tibet in the next phase. The meeting formulated more preferential policies to provide Tibet with stronger support, and embodied the great concern of the State Council for the work in Tibet, and special care for all ethnic groups in Tibet. The development measures formulated at the meeting have gained great popularity among the people, because they suit the national conditions, Tibet's reality and the fundamental interests of people of all ethnic groups in Tibet. The meeting indicates that Tibet, now at a new historical stage, is facing a very rare development opportunity. The Fifth Tibet Work Symposium, as an important milestone, will definitely promote Tibet's leapfrog development and lasting stability.

The Fifth Tibet Work Symposium stressed efforts to develop Tibet in accordance with the region's resource conditions, industrial foundation, and the national strategic requirements by making overall plans and scientific arrangements, giving priority to industries with regional features and strategic pillar industries with a competitive edge, and increasing self-development capacity by easing the bottleneck effect of poor infrastructure and energy shortage on economic development. The meeting decided to actively implement the development strategy of "upgrading primary industry, developing key secondary industries and greatly advancing tertiary industry." The meeting enriched the spirit of Tibet's economic development strategy, and further clarified the tasks and requirements.

Tibet's strategy for economic development consists of five key points:

First, making great efforts to develop the economy, and realizing quicker, better and bigger development.

Second, vigorously carrying forward social construction and improving public services and social management.

Third, ensuring the people's livelihood and improving the people's living standard.

Fourth, vigorously improving ecological civilization, and enhancing the capacity to achieve sustainable development.

Fifth, implementing the principle that the cadres and the people of all ethnic groups in Tibet should work arduously to develop Tibet, under the care of the central government and with the support of the entire country, and increasing assistance to Tibet, and ensuring the realization of a well-off society there in an all-round way by 2020.

41. What are the main problems in Tibet's social and economic development? What are Tibet's development goals in the next period?

Since Tibet's Democratic Reform more than 50 years ago, the people of all ethnic groups in Tibet have worked arduously and made concerted efforts to realize its leapfrog social and economic development, and make remarkable achievements in all social undertakings. With the care of the Central People's Government and the help of all the Chinese people, Tibet has witnessed dramatic changes. However, due to various historical, natural and social reasons, Tibet is a less-developed region in general. The tasks of developing the social productive forces and meet the growing material and cultural needs of the people remain difficult. Tibet's social and economic development is bedeviled by the following problems at the current stage: Despite a steady increase in the total economic volume, there is still no fundamental change in the fact that Tibet's development started late and on a poor foundation, and the region is still relatively underdeveloped; some urban and rural people, especially some farmers and herdsmen, are still living difficult lives; problems such as backward social undertakings, poor public services in the farming and pastoral areas, poor social security, uneven social and economic development, and unbalanced development between the urban and rural areas still exist. These are the most prominent problems we have to address in Tibet's social and economic development.

The Fifth Tibet Work Symposium provided guidelines and made arrangements for the realization of Tibet's leapfrog development and lasting stability in the new situation. In accordance with the spirit of the Fifth Tibet Work Symposium, in the next period, while pushing development forward, more attention should be paid to improving the living standard of the farmers and herdsmen, achieving coordinated social and economic development, increasing self-development capacity, enhancing capability and balanced development of basic public services in the region, protecting the plateau's ecological environment, expanding co-operation and exchanges between Tibet and other parts of China, building a mechanism for better economic and social development, and realizing the harmonious development of economic growth, affluence, ecological soundness, social stability, and the progress of civilization. Efforts should be made to reach the following goals: By 2015, the gap between the per capita net income of Tibet's farmers and herdsmen and the nation's average is to be significantly narrowed; basic public services notably enhanced; ecological environment further improved, and Tibet will have a more solid foundation for the building of a well-off society in an all-round way. By 2020 the per capita net income of Tibet's farmers and herdsmen will be very near to the nation's average, and the region's public service capacity will be near to the nation's average capacity; there will be comprehensively improved infrastructures, notable progress in building ecological security, substantially enhanced self-development capacity, and ensured success in building a well-off society in an all-round way.

42. Who are the biggest beneficiaries of the central government's support for Tibet?

The central government has enacted many preferential policies for Tibet and provided strong financial, material and human resource support since Tibet's Democratic Reform 50 years ago. In reviewing the history of development of the Tibet Autonomous Region over the past half-century, we can see that its economic development has gone through three main historical stages.

1959-1965: from the democratic reform to the formal establishment of the People's Government of the Tibet Autonomous Region

The 1959 Democratic Reform abolished feudal serfdom, and fundamentally reformed the ownership of the means of production, which prompted Tibet's rapid economic development. As demanded by the serfs, who accounted for the overwhelming majority of Tibet's population, 95% or more of the land, livestock and other major means of production in Tibet that had been owned by the feudal upper class (5% of the population) were distributed among the former serfs; private ownership of farmers and herdsmen was set up; and policies in favor of stable development were carried out. The reform of the ownership of the means of production greatly liberated the productive forces, and Tibet thereby saw unprecedentedly rapid economic growth. In the six years from the 1959 Democratic Reform to 1965, when the Tibet Autonomous Region was established, Tibet's economic aggregate rocketed to 327 million yuan, with an annual growth rate of 11.1%. Tibet's economy had entered a stage of rapid development.

1965-1984: from the formal establishment of the People's Government of the Tibet Autonomous Region to the adoption of reform and opening up in 1978

After the People's Government of the Tibet Autonomous Region was formally established in 1965, the central government adopted policies to give economic support to Tibet to guarantee its stable economic development. In 1984 the central government held the Second Tibet Work Symposium in Beijing. This meeting decided to continue the special preferential policies in Tibet's rural areas. In the same year, Tibet's government declared that it would carry out the policy of opening to inland provinces and foreign countries. In this period Tibet's economy experienced relatively stable growth, with an annual growth rate of 7.82%.

1984-present: from the adoption of the reform and opening-up policies to the present

Tibet's reform and opening up, which started in 1984, provided strong support for the region's economic development. In the meantime, the central government's policies and financial support, coordinated assistance from more developed inland provinces and cities and the joint efforts of the people of all the ethnic groups in Tibet combined to lift Tibet to the stage of the fastest economic growth in its history. The economic aggregate soared from 1.368 billion yuan in 1984 to 44.136 billion yuan in 2009, an increase of 11.3 times within 25 years calculated at comparable prices, and the annual growth rate reached the high level of 10.5%.

To promote better and faster economic development in Tibet, the central government held the Fourth Tibet Work Symposium in 2001. The meeting decided upon 117 state-invested projects, involving a total funding of 31.2 billion yuan; moreover, the central government also provided 38 billion yuan in financial subsidies, while 70 assistance projects and aid funds to Tibet from around the country totaled over 3 billion yuan. Driven by such huge funding, the economic aggregate of Tibet rose from 13.916 billion yuan in 2001 to 44.136 billion yuan in 2009, with a high annual growth rate of 12.4%. In 2006 the per capita GDP of Tibet exceeded 10,000 yuan.

Investment has had a remarkable influence on the economic growth of Tibet. From 1959 to 2009 Tibet's investment in fixed assets grew from 29 million yuan to 37.942 billion yuan, and the annual growth rate reached 15.2%. In 1985, the second year of Tibet's opening up, the investment in fixed assets accounted for 42.2% of that year's GDP, at least 10 percentage points more than 1959. Since then, Tibet's investment in fixed assets has grown by a big margin, and its proportion in the GDP has remained at a relatively high level. In each of the ten years from 1984 to 1994 the proportion of Tibet's investment in fixed assets in its GDP was more than 40%. This figure rose to 66% in 1995, and dropped to between 45% and 47% in the 1996-1998 period. After that, Tibet accelerated its investment in fixed assets. In the six years from 2003 to 2009 the proportion of Tibet's investment in fixed assets in its GDP was more than 75%, over 20 percentage points higher than the national average.

As China's national strength has steadily increased since the introduction of the policies of reform and opening up, the central government has paid more attention and offered more support to the Tibet Autonomous Region, which is located in the border area in southwest China and the economic development of which traditionally lagged behind other areas of the country. To accelerate Tibet's development, the central government held five Tibet Work Symposiums in Beijing in 1980, 1984, 1994, 2001 and 2010, respectively, providing more financial transfer payments and more investment in key projects for Tibet, bringing into being a framework for all places in China to provide assistance to Tibet.

Since the Democratic Reform in 1959, and especially since the adoption of the policies of reform and opening up in 1978, Tibet has witnessed remarkable economic development. Nonetheless, for various reasons, many challenges remain, including the high cost of economic and social development, underdeveloped market, unbalanced economic and social development in urban and rural areas, low market competitiveness of farmers and herdsmen, and underdeveloped human capital. These are the long-term challenges Tibet has to address in order to achieve sound economic development.

But it is important to point out that most of the investment that local governments in Tibet use to develop their economy is not from self-accumulation or market allocation, but from the central government's financial transfer payments and input for various projects in Tibet, and assistance from more-developed inland provinces and cities.

The central government's transfer payments to Tibet amounted to 201.9 billion yuan between 1959 and 2008, and the figure totaled more than 154.1 billion yuan between 2001 and 2008, making up 93.7% of Tibet's financial revenue in the same period. This means that for every 100 yuan Tibet spent, over 90 yuan came from the central government.

The central government is now drawing up the 12th Five-Year Plan for the development of Tibet, and its basic ideas have been determined: the central government's financial transfer payment to Tibet during the 12th Five-Year Plan will double the amount during the 11th Five-Year Plan, to reach or possibly exceed 300 billion yuan. In addition, the central government will increase its input into the Tibetan-inhabited areas in Qinghai, Sichuan, Guansu and Yunnan, which will undoubtedly enter a stage of accelerated development.

Facts and figures demonstrate that the central government and inland provinces have provided great support for the development of Tibet, which is now in a golden period of development. The claim that "the central government receives more from Tibet than it gives to the region" is groundless.

The Tibet Autonomous Region is a minority region with the Tibetans as the majority. The Tibetans and other ethnic minority groups constitute more than 95% of the region's total population. With the care of the central government and the support of the entire country, people of all ethnic groups in Tibet have been making concerted efforts to achieve remarkable economic and social development, and continuously improve the local people's living standard since the peaceful liberation of Tibet. The Tibetans and other ethnic minorities, who enjoy the fruits of Tibet's social and economic development, are the main beneficiaries.

In recent years, assistance projects funded by the central government, inland provinces and enterprises have been more and more in favor of the farming and pastoral areas in Tibet, and have proved effective. However, we have to admit that due to personal limitations and slowness to adapt to market competition, some people have difficulty to find jobs and are still under economic strain. In order to help Tibet's urban residents, farmers and herdsmen find jobs, the regional government has taken effective measures, such as improving training and information services, and employment recommendation. By the end of March 2010 Tibet's registered urban unemployed numbered 20,000, showing an unemployment rate below 4.3%. Tibet also became the first region in China to eliminate zero-employment families.

43. What is the state of Tibet's socio-economic development? What economic achievements has Tibet made since the Democratic Reform?

In 1951, when Tibet was peacefully liberated, its total population was 1.1409 million; its economy featured absolute domination of agriculture and animal husbandry, with very limited commerce and handicraft industry. The total output value of Tibet was 129 million yuan, among which the value of the primary, secondary (the building sector) and tertiary industries stood at 126 million yuan, 100 thousand yuan and 3 million yuan, respectively. The per capita output value was 114 yuan. In 1959, the first year of the Democratic Reform, the total output value was 174 million yuan and the per capita output value was 142 yuan. The total figure rose to 327 million yuan in 1965, when the Tibet Autonomous Region was founded, with the per capita figure increasing to 241 yuan. Since then, and especially after the Third Plenary Session of the Eleventh CPC Central Committee in 1978 and the Third Tibet Work Symposium in 1994, Tibet entered a stage of rapid development. Under the care of the central government and with the support of all the Chinese people, especially with the coordinated assistance provided by 15 provinces and cities, Tibet realized rapid socio-economic development and industrial structure optimization, and the people's living standard improved greatly. In 1980 Tibet's total output value reached 867 million yuan, among which, the value of the primary, secondary and tertiary industries stood at 464 million yuan, 218 million yuan and 185 million yuan, respectively. The per capita output value reached 471 yuan. In its industrial structure, primary industry was the largest, secondary industry took the middle place and tertiary industry was the smallest one in terms of their weight in the region's total output value. In 2000 the region's GDP increased more than 30 times compared with 1951, to reach 11.78 billion yuan, among which, the value of the primary, secondary and tertiary industries stood at 3.639 billion yuan, 2.705 billion yuan and 5.437 billion yuan, respectively. The industrial structure formed a pattern with tertiary industry as the largest, primary industry taking the middle place and secondary industry as the smallest one in terms of their weight in the region's GDP. Under the care of the central government and with the support of all the Chinese people, the Chinese government invested a total of 54 billion yuan in fixed assets in Tibet, provided 40 billion yuan in financial support and subsidies, and carried out a group of key projects including the Qinghai-Tibet Railway during the Tenth Five-Year Plan. All of these efforts vigorously promoted Tibet's economic development.

In 2005 Tibet's total output value reached 25.121 billion yuan. The ratio of the value of Tibet's primary, secondary and tertiary industries changed from 97.7%: 0: 2.3% in 1951 to

19.1%: 25.3%: 55.6% in 2005. In 2009 Tibet further upgraded its industrial structure, as the total output value reached 44.136 billion yuan, and the ratio between the value of the primary, secondary and tertiary industries was 14.5%: 30.9%: 54.6%. The total economic volume of Tibet maintained a growth rate above 12% for seven consecutive years. The per capita output value exceeded 10,000 yuan for the first time in 2006, and reached 15,295 yuan in 2009.

Tibet's infrastructure construction made an important break-through on July 1, 2006, when the Qinghai-Tibet Railway went into operation, attracting worldwide attention and ending Tibet's history of being without railways. In the same period, Tibet put Nyingchi Airport into operation, completed the construction of power stations including the Shiquanhe Hydropower Station, and renovated key roads. From 2001 to 2005 Tibet completed road construction projects at a total cost of 14.692 billion yuan, and renovated roads totaling 2,000 km, including the Qinghai-Tibet Highway, Sichuan-Tibet Highway and China-Nepal Highway. In the 11th Five-Year Plan, which began in 2006, the central govern-ment decided to spend 7.78 billion yuan in 180 construction proj-ects in Tibet in the five years.

In 2009 Tibet completed highway construction projects at a total cost of 6.062 billion yuan, registering a growth rate of 34.65% compared with 2008. The total highway mileage had reached 53,845 km by the end of 2009, 2,531 km more than in

2008. The mileage of paved road had reached 3,279 km, 384 km more than that in 2008. So far, 67% of the counties in Tibet have access to asphalt roads, and 97.95% of the townships and 80.25% of the villages have access to highways.

In 2009 China scaled up highway construction in Tibet. The number of projects, total cost, the number of people benefited and the effect on economic development were all unprecedented. According to official statistics, road construction contributed 1.2 percentage points to Tibet's economic growth rate, or 9.6% of the growth. In that year Tibet started 19 key highway construction projects, including the highway that would connect Lhasa and Gongkar Airport, and National Highway G214 (Chamdo-Pangda Airport section), and completed and put into use 11 projects, including National Highway G317 line (Jomda-Thopa section) and National Highway G219 (Montser-Barga section). In the same year Tibet started 95 rural highway projects at a total cost of 780 million yuan and a total mileage of 4,081 km, to help 19 townships and 213 large villages gain access to highways. At the end of 2009 the region's total number of civilian motor vehicles reached 199,000, an increase of 3.1% over the same period of 2008.

Now Tibet's road network has formed the pattern of "three longitudes and three latitudes" with Lhasa as its center. The network connects Tibet with Sichuan, Yunnan and Qinghai provinces and the Xinjiang Uygur Autonomous Region, and crosses the border to connect Tibet with India and Nepal. Tibet has basically completed its road network, featuring provincial highway linkage, and connection between prefecture-level cities, counties and townships, upgraded highway technology standards, and greatly improved road conditions.

Tibet's posts and telecommunications have seen steady growth, as the region provides more investments, scales up the industry and upgrades information network technologies.

Tibet's telecommunications industry, making use of the advantages of comprehensive information services, has bridged the urban-rural digital gap, promoted socio-economic development, and completed such important projects as "optical cable connection in all counties," "telephone communication coverage in all townships," "fax connection in all townships," "optical cable connection in all townships" and "telephone communication coverage in all villages." At present, telephones, mobile phones and the Internet are rapidly entering the possession of ordinary families. Modern information technologies provide great convenience to people of all ethnic groups in their work and daily life. The information superhighways have also helped Tibet to rapidly develop its various social undertakings.

In recent years Tibet has carried out postal reforms to accelerate the commercialized operation of postal services, and opened new fields by vigorously developing its electronic postal services. The region has also accelerated its postal modernization by further enhancing the three major postal functions, namely information transfer, logistics and fund flows. Newly developed fields such as mail advertisements, postal etiquette services, mail-orders and postal savings are also continuously increasing the value of postal services. In 2009 the value of postal services reached 169 million yuan, an increase of 14.3% over the previous year; the business income reached 176 million yuan, an increase of 17.14% over the previous year; and the volume of postal savings reached 38.18 million yuan, an increase of 23.3% over the previous year. Tibet is still improving its postal services to better satisfy the needs of its inhabitants and make people's life more convenient.

In 1959 Tibet had only 276 telephones, mostly located in large and medium-sized cities like Lhasa. The value of postal and telecommunications services then totaled only 990,000 yuan. Now, Tibet has formed an advanced communications network covering every part of the region, with Lhasa as the center, providing services through optical cables and satellite transmitters, and combining program-controlled exchanges and satellite, digital and mobile communications. Telecommunications services have expanded to cover mobile phones, video-conferencing and computer network. The expanded services facilitate economic development and satisfy the people's various needs. The value of telecommunications services in Tibet reached 5.043 billion yuan in 2009, up 25.3% over the previous year. Now Tibet's telephone exchange capacity has reached 419,900 lines. There are 539,300 telephone subscribers in the region, with the urban and rural telephone subscribers numbering 512,100 and 272,000 households, respectively.

In recent years Tibet has also achieved rapid development in mobile communications, as mobile communications providers expand mobile phone subscribers and the mobile communications market, and promote short-message services and the activity of "getting free mobile phones by making advance payments for services." In 2009 Tibet's total value of mobile telecommunications network services reached 469 million yuan, an increase of 136.7% over the previous year; the total mobile phone exchange capacity reached 1.89 million lines, an increase of 625,000 lines over the previous year; mobile phone subscribers totaled 1.2551 million, an increase of 419,900 subscribers over the previous year; and there are 62 telephones for every 100 people.

China Telecom will further increase its investment in Tibet's telecommunications and information-based infrastructure, promote Tibet's informationization, and provide a complete basic information network, information application services and communications support.

In the five years following 2009, it is estimated, China Telecom's fixed assets value in the region will reach at least 2.5 billion yuan in total. About 85% of townships and 60% of large villages in Tibet will be brought into the broadband information network by 2011. As an advanced information network reaches remote villages in the farming and pastoral areas, information technology will make the life of farmers and herdsmen more convenient.

Tibet is a region dominated by agriculture and animal husbandry. However, these sectors remain weak due to historical reasons and harsh natural conditions. Most of the agricultural and livestock products are consumed within the region because poor transportation conditions prevent them from entering the national market. Therefore, the completion and operation of the Qinghai-Tibet Railway provides an unprecedented opportunity for Tibet to expand the market for its agricultural products.

In 2009 Tibet's agricultural output reached 905.75 million yuan-worth, and its output of animal husbandry reached 4.4288 billion yuan-worth; the region's total crop output was 905,300 tons, of which 57,700 tons was rapeseed and 551,100 tons was vegetables. Tibet had 23.24 million head of domestic animals in stock at the end of 2009, including 6.53 million herd of cattle and 15.84 million herd of sheep. In the same year, the output of pork, beef and mutton reached 255,200 tons, an increase of 4.3% over the previous year; and the milk output reached 294,300 tons.

In recent years, farmers have begun to tailor their production to the needs of the market. For example, many farmers are increasing the acreage of rapeseed and high-quality highland barley, for which there is a growing demand and rising prices, and at the same time are reducing the area of winter wheat. Herdsmen are reducing the number of horses they raise, which need large areas of grassland and a lot of feedstuffs but are of little value nowadays. Farmers and herdsmen have also profited greatly from the price rises of most agricultural and livestock products. For instance, in the time of the planned economy a kilo of yak meat cost less than one yuan, but now people have to pay more than 40 yuan for the same amount of meat. A robust yak could even be swapped for a hand-guided tractor. As a result, more and more farmers and herdsmen are transferring extra products and labor to where the needs of the market lie.

Besides rapid and sustained economic development, Tibet has also achieved comprehensive progress in various social undertakings. As we know, the old Tibet didn't have any schools in the modern sense, and the illiteracy rate was 95%. But since Tibet's peaceful liberation the central government has paid special attention to and provided strong support for Tibet's educational undertakings. An education system with local characteristics has taken shape – from preschool to higher, vocational and adult education. At present, the local population receives an average 6.3 years of education. For adults without school education, especially those under the age of 50, literacy courses and evening classes are provided, reducing the illiteracy rate to under 2.4% so far. In light of the needs of the labor market in Tibet, training courses in practical skills and techniques are also offered to farmers and herdsmen, covering areas such as farming, animal husbandry and machinery maintenance. Training courses are also offered to surplus laborers from farming and pastoral areas to help them obtain employment.

In addition to improving its own school conditions, Tibet has started to open classes and schools in the hinterland by using the local superior teaching resources. Since 1985 some 18 mainland provinces and cities have provided a total of 576 million yuan for Tibet's education, and renovated over 300 kindergartens, and primary and middle schools in 74 counties in Tibet. Since 1985 the central government has set up Tibetan classes and schools in 20 inland provinces and cities covering all levels of education from junior middle school to university.

While steadily promoting modern education, Tibet attaches special importance to Tibetan-language education. The Constitution of the People's Republic of China and the Law of the People's Republic of China on Regional Ethnic Autonomy both explicitly stipulate that the ethnic minorities' freedom to use and develop their own languages is guaranteed. The Regulations of the Tibet Autonomous Region on the Study, Use and Development of the Tibetan Language, revised in 2002, reinforced the legal status of the Tibetan language in Tibet's educational endeavors.

The total education expenditure of the autonomous region in 2009 was 6.107 billion yuan, an increase of 29.7%. In the same year, Tibet's six regular higher education institutions enrolled 9,248 students, including 228 postgraduate students and 9,020 junior college students and graduate students; the total number of students in those institutions was 30,853, including 589 postgraduate students and 30,264 junior college students and graduate students; and 8,594 students graduated, including 140 postgraduates and 8,454 graduates. That same year, the six secondary vocational schools enrolled 11,038 students and 3,603 graduated, altogether there were 21,357 students in such schools. Tibet has 118 middle schools, including 15 senior high schools, nine combined junior and senior high schools, and 94 junior high schools. The senior high schools received 13,884 students and 13,312 graduated. There were 38,383 students studying in such schools. The junior high schools received 50,042 students and 42,401 graduated. There were 143,187 students studying in such schools. The 884 primary schools received 53,682 students and 50,850 graduated. There were 305,235 students learning in such schools. The special schools received 11 students, and altogether there were 200 students studying in such schools. By the end of 2009 a total of 16,068 children were in kindergartens, an increase of 1,401 compared to the previous year. The school-age children enrollment rate of the autonomous region reached 98.8%, an increase of 0.3 percentage points over the previous year.

Before the 1959 Democratic Reform Tibet had only three official Tibetan medical institutions and a few poorly equipped private clinics. There were less than 400 medical staff – a rate of 0.4 per 1,000 people. Following the Democratic Reform the central government adopted special health policies for the Tibet Autonomous Region, under which individual health savings accounts are supplemented by government subsidies in urban areas, and free medical services are provided in farming and pastoral areas. From 1959 to 2008 the country allocated special funds totaling over 1.8 billion yuan for the development of Tibet's medical and health work, providing an annual medical subsidy of more than 20 million yuan to the local farmers and herdsmen. By the end of 2008 there were 1,339 medical institutions in Tibet, over 20 times the number in 1959; the total number of hospital beds was increased from 480 in 1959 to 7,127 in 2008 – 2.50 beds per 1,000 people in 2008 and 2.11 more than that in 1959. The number of hospital beds and medical staff per 1,000 people in Tibet is higher than the national average and even higher than that of middle-income countries.

Statistics show that in 2009 Tibet's total medical expenditure was 2.184 billion yuan, an increase of 33.6%. There were 763 hospitals and health clinics, 81 disease prevention and control centers (health control agencies), 57 maternal and child care service centers, clinics and stations in the autonomous region, providing 5,368 hospital beds among the total of 8,553 ward beds, and 3,395 medical practitioners among the total of 10,047 medical technical staff. The average medical subsidy for farmers

and herdsmen was 140 yuan, of which 125 yuan was in the form
of a central government financial subsidy and 15 yuan as an autonomous region subsidy.

44. What is the livelihood of the Tibetan people like?

The central government always attaches great importance to the people's livelihood. The government makes it a primary task to improve farmers' and herdsmen's living standards, and increase their incomes, and makes sure that people of all ethnic groups can enjoy the fruits of the reform and development. The Fifth Tibet Work Symposium demanded that the people's material and cultural lives be constantly enriched, because improving the people's livelihood is the purpose and goal of the work in Tibet.

Now Tibet has basically built a well-off society, and greatly improved the livelihood of the people of all ethnic groups, more than 50 years after Tibet's Democratic Reform and some 30 years after the reform and opening-up policies were introduced nationwide. In 2009 Tibet's per capita output value reached 15,295 yuan, and the per capita income of the farmers and herdsmen reached 3,532 yuan, registering a double-digit growth rate for seven consecutive years.

The regional government has increased its spending on housing projects and improved the housing conditions for low-income urban and rural families through building low-rent houses, temporary houses and economically affordable houses, providing subsidies for those who rent houses, and improving the housing system. Through advancing the "new countryside" program and carrying out the housing project, the government provided houses for 1.2 million farmers and herdsmen from 230,000 families in 2009. In the same year, the per capita housing space for urban residents in Tibet reached 33.83 sq m, and that for farmers and herdsmen reached 23.62 sq m.

In 2009 the regional government invested 786 million yuan for building houses for 59,637 households, benefiting 330,000 people. In the same year, the regional government also invested 298 million yuan to consolidate and reconstruct rural houses to make them safe from earthquakes. At the same time, the government speeded up the construction of comprehensive support projects, such as provision of safe drinking water for people and livestock in farming and pastoral areas, complete coverage of water, electricity, road networks, telecommunications, radio and television, and postal services, and replacing traditional firewood with methane as fuel for heating and cooking. Today, refrigerators, color TVs, washing machines, motorcycles and mobile phones have entered ordinary families. Computers and automobiles are also on the shopping lists of many Tibetan people.

45. What are the obstacles to Tibet's economic development?

There are still many problems in Tibet's socio-economic development: First, due to Tibet's poor natural conditions, low productivity of farming and animal husbandry, low added value of agricultural and livestock products, and long distances from the main markets, the task of steadily increasing the farmers' and herdsmen's income, and improving their living standards remains an arduous one; second, the region still lacks revenue sources, and its self-development and self-accumulation capacities are still low; third, poor infrastructure, especially backward energy and transportation facilities are still hampering the region's economic development; fourth, social undertakings and public services are still underdeveloped; fifth, the Dalai Lama's separatists' sabotage is still a major factor in hampering the region's development, and the struggle against the separatist force is still arduous. All of the above difficulties and challenges reflect the region's long accumulated contradictions. Those problems are development problems and urgently need to be solved in the course of our future work in Tibet.

46. Do Tibet's farmers and herdsmen enjoy any preferential policies? How is Tibet's agriculture and animal husbandry?

Since Tibet's peaceful liberation more than 50 years ago, and especially since China's introduction of the reform and opening-up policies more than 30 years ago, the central government and the government of the Tibet Autonomous Region have greatly assisted the region's economic development and the living standard of farmers and herdsmen by adopting preferential policies to rehabilitate the farming and pastoral areas. Today, most farmers and herdsmen are comparatively well off.

The government has also made following preferential policies for Tibet's farmers and herdsmen: (1) In farming areas, "land should be used by individual farm households for their own production, a policy which will be kept unchanged for a long time to come;" in pastoral areas, "livestock should be owned and raised by individual herdsman households, a policy which will be kept unchanged for a long time to come;" "the pasture should be publicly owned, and contracted by herdsmen for their own production." (2) Tibet, as a special region, is given full support and more poverty alleviation funds from the central government. (3) The government exempts Tibet's township enterprises from income taxes, to encourage their development. (4) The government provides financial subsidies for purchasing agricultural production necessities such as pesticides, fertilizer, and agricultural machinery, and purchases grain and edible oil from farmers at preferential prices. (5) The government provides free medical treatment in farming and pastoral areas. It also pays the food, board and tuition fees for children receiving compulsory education.

Agriculture and animal husbandry are Tibet's pillar industries. The regional governments at all levels pay special attention to the development of agriculture and animal husbandry, and have formulated many policies to accelerate their development. These policies focus on increasing farmers and herdsmen's incomes and improving the efficiency of agriculture and animal husbandry, seek to increase grain productivity, actively accelerate the structural adjustment of farming and animal husbandry, speed up the development of animal husbandry, township enterprises, diversified production, non-agricultural economic sectors and the industrialized operation of agriculture. The policies also vigorously promote technological advances and innovation in the field of agriculture and animal husbandry.

In 2001 the region reduced the acreage of winter and spring wheat, and increased the area of crops with higher demand, such as highland barley, corn, beans and rapeseed. The year 2001 was the 14th consecutive bumper harvest year for Tibet. In that year the production of grain and rapeseed reached 980,000 tons and

45,000 tons, respectively, much more than in the previous year, and over five times as much as in 1959. The farmers' average net income increased 5.9% compared with the previous year. In 2002 the crop production structure was further optimized; the acreage of cash crops and forage crops was further increased, and the total grain production increased 0.2% over the previous year to reach 984,000 tons. Township enterprises in Tibet were also thriving in 2007, when they grew to 965 in number, with 52,000 employees and a total output value of 2.35 billion yuan.[1] At present, there are 17 pilot areas of "enterprise plus farmers" industrialized operation, which are seeing growing economic benefits. Traditional quality products such as Gurum tsamba (a type of bread), Liangamu tsamba and Emagang potatoes, their trade marks already registered, are very popular on the market.

Tibet has increased the output of agriculture and animal husbandry by further adjusting its crop production structure and building industrial bases with regional features, such as the Shannan garlic production base and Panam vegetable production base.

Tibet is a region dominated by agriculture and animal husbandry. However, these sectors remain weak due to historical reasons and harsh natural conditions. Most of the agricultural and livestock products are consumed within the region because poor transportation conditions prevent them from entering the national market. Therefore, the completion and operation of the Qinghai-Tibet Railway provides an unprecedented opportunity for Tibet to expand the market for its agricultural products.

In 2009 Tibet's agricultural output reached 905.75 million yuan-worth, and its output of animal husbandry reached 4.4288 billion yuan-worth; the region's total crop output was 905,300 tons, of which 57,700 tons was rapeseed and 551,100 tons was vegetables. Tibet had 23.24 million head of domestic animals in stock at the end of 2009, including 6.53 million herd of cattle and 15.84 million herd of sheep. In the same year, the output of pork, beef and mutton reached 255,200 tons, an increase of 4.3% over the previous year; and the milk output reached 294,300 tons.

In recent years, farmers have begun to tailor their production to the needs of the market. For example, many farmers are increasing the acreage of rapeseed and high-quality highland barley, for which there is a growing demand and rising prices, and at the same time are reducing the area of winter wheat. Herdsmen are reducing the number of horses they raise, which need large areas of grassland and a lot of feedstuffs but are of little value nowadays. Farmers and herdsmen have also profited greatly from the price rises of most agricultural and livestock products. For instance, in the time of the planned economy a kilo of yak meat cost less than one yuan, but now people have to pay more than 40 yuan for the same amount of meat. A robust yak could even be swapped for a hand-guided tractor. As a result, more and more farmers and herdsmen are transferring extra products and labor to where the needs of the market lie.

In 2009 notable progress was made in Tibet's work of improving the people's living standard through afforestation, increasing farmers' and herdsmen's incomes by a total of 650 million yuan, up 62% over the previous year's figure. A total of 742,800 *mu* (a unit of area equal to 1/6 of an acre) of land was afforested in 2009, including 296,100 *mu* in key afforestation areas, 47,800 *mu* in areas around Lhasa, 95,900 *mu* in sandstorm-prevention afforestation areas, and 150,000 *mu* in areas for returning farmland for forest and afforestation on barren mountains.

Note:

[1] See "Glorious History: Great Changes of Tibet's Agriculture and Animal Husbandry in the 30 Years after the Reform and Opening up," *Tibet Daily*, November 19, 2008.

47. What progress is Tibet making in its housing project for farmers and herdsmen? How will the project improve employment, medical care and education for the farming and pastoral areas?

Around 80% of Tibet's population lives in farming and pastoral areas, and the primary task of the regional government is to improve the living and production conditions for the farmers and herdsmen. Supported by government finances, social funds, private investment and Tibet-aid funds, in January 2006 the regional government started to carry out the new "socialist countryside" program, with emphasis on housing for farmers and herdsmen, aiming to provide comfortable and affordable houses for 80% of the farmers and herdsmen with poor housing conditions. By the end of 2009 governments at various levels in the Tibet Autonomous Region had invested a total of 3.44 billion yuan to house more than 1.2 million farmers and herdsmen from 230,000 households – one year ahead of schedule. At the same time, the governments also supported the housing projects by simultaneously improving water and electricity supply, road networks, telecommunications, and radio and television availability. In 2010 more efforts were pledged to provide comfortable houses for the other 20% of the farmers and herdsmen with poor housing conditions.

The project is greatly improving the housing conditions of farmers and herdsmen, and elevating their production and living standards. At the same time, the regional government has increased its funds earmarked for the improvement of medical care, education and employment, building of medical care organizations to cover all urban and rural areas, establishing a medical system in farming and pastoral areas and providing free medical care for all farmers and herdsmen. The regional government has also greatly increased its subsidies to pay for the food, board and tuition for children receiving compulsory education in farming and pastoral areas. More than 270,000 students receive an average subsidy of 1,800 per year. In 2009 the regional government invested 830 million yuan to develop agriculture and animal husbandry, provide training courses in science, practical skills and techniques, organize labor transfer, and further increase farmers and herdsmen's ability to support themselves.

48. What is the position of social security in Tibet?

In 2005 the people's government of Tibet provided allowances to farmers and herdsmen with an annual net income below 300 yuan. Since 2006 a system of minimum subsistence allowances for rural residents has been instituted across Tibet, and the poverty line for allowances has increased by a big margin to cover families with an average annual per capita income of less than 800 yuan. Some 230,000 rural families have benefited from this policy. Since 2003 the regional government has several times raised the allowance for elderly people living alone, the disabled who have lost the ability to work and minors with no source of income. The annual allowance per person has been raised from 588 yuan in the past to 1,600 yuan. In 2009 the regional government again adjusted the poverty line for minimum subsistence allowance, raising the minimum annual per capita income from 850 yuan to 1,100 yuan for rural residents, and from 260 yuan to 310 yuan for urban residents.

In 2009 the region vigorously promoted its social security programs. The social security and employment spending reached 3.23 billion yuan in 2009, up 15.8% over the previous year. Social security coverage further expanded to include a total of 721,000 people. After the March 14 Incident, the government offered a total of 19.365 million yuan in subsidies to businesses, industries and employers who had suffered from the rioting, in the form of unemployment, medical and house renovation aid, rental subsidy and discount loans, and successfully helped the damaged industries out of difficulties. The government also helped enterprises overcome the impact of the global financial crisis, and allocated 39.8934 million yuan in the form of subsidies for enterprises in difficulty, and social security and job subsidies. On March 28 the central government provided 530 million yuan-worth of aid to Tibet to commemorate the 50th anniversary of the liberation of the serfs there.

All pensions for the region's elderly are being paid through social service institutions in time and in full. By the end of 2009 some 88,000 employees were covered by basic pension insurance; 88,000 employees by unemployment insurance; 69,000 by work injury insurance; 125,000 by maternity insurance; and 220,000 urban employees and 131,000 urban residents by basic medical insurance. (Another 39,000 urban residents were covered by the medical system applied in the farming and pastoral areas, among whom 18,000 were students of junior colleges and technical secondary schools.)

The regional government issued a total of 99.2137 million yuan as minimum subsistence allowances to 39,415 urban residents, and a total of 112.6 million yuan to 230,000 rural residents. At the end of the year there were 205 social welfare organizations of various types, with 5,131 beds. These organizations sheltered 3,696 elderly persons without family, disabled children and orphans. The region sold 278 million welfare lottery tickets in 2009, raising 86.78 million yuan in social welfare funds.

Tibet also made efforts to boost employment and reemployment, and increased the graduate employment rate. The regional government took various measures to address unemployment issues, including recruiting civil servants through open public examinations, and promoting market employment. In this endeavor 20,000 more job opportunities were created, including jobs for 10,000 graduates, and the problem of zero-employment families was eliminated. The registered urban unemployment rate was under 4%.

49. How is Tibet doing in poverty alleviation?

It is a firm goal of the CPC and the people's governments at all levels to make sure that the Tibetan people can live a comfortable life. Abolishing feudal serfdom, and carrying out Democratic Reform and the reform and opening-up policies all serve this purpose. Since the regional government formulated and implemented the Poverty Alleviation Program in the Tibet Autonomous Region in 1996, the regional government has adhered to poverty alleviation through development. The regional government attaches primary importance to developing crop production and animal husbandry, improving the production and living conditions of poverty-stricken people. The regional government has also raised funds from various sources, increased poverty-alleviation investment, established the pair-up poverty-alleviation between a poor place and a relatively well-off place, and sought help from all walks of life and international organizations to support poverty alleviation in Tibet. Meanwhile, the regional government pays close attention to the ecological environment, and promotes sustainable development in the poverty-stricken areas.

The poverty alleviation measures through development have greatly changed the situation of the poverty-stricken areas, and greatly improved the comprehensive productivity of agriculture and animal husbandry. By the end of 2002 the government had solved the problem of food and clothing for most of the 480,000 people in the 18 poverty-stricken counties. Most of these people are on their way to a well-off life, and the "Eight-Seven" Rural Alleviation Program ("Eight" here means 80 million rural population living in poverty, and "Seven" means 7 years. The purpose of this Progam was to alleviate 80 million poverty-stricken rural people within 7 years.) has proved successful. The region's task has now shifted to improving the living standard of relatively poor people.

During the period of the "Baqi" Rural Alleviation Program (1996-2001), the regional government spent a total of more than 1.14 billion yuan (0.93 billion yuan from the central government), set up 1,100 poverty-alleviation development projects, involving total funds of 1.43 billion yuan (including 1.15 billion yuan from central government), upgraded 3.12 million *mu* of middle- and low-yield fields and 238,000 *mu* of natural, cultivated and enclosed pastures, build 180 irrigation channels with a total length of more than 6,000 km, improved irrigation on 2.16 million *mu* of farmland and pastures, built, expanded or rebuilt 25 hydropower stations, with an installed capacity of 5,805 kw, built 6,000 km of country roads and roads for draft animals, and 137 bridges, installed 3,596 items of solar lighting equipment, and constructed 480 drinking water projects to solve the water problems for 96,000 people and 1.85 million head of livestock.

In 2002 the central government allocated 305 million yuan for poverty alleviation in Tibet. It arranged 256 projects to improve the Tibetan people's living and production conditions, including rural energy development, farmland water conservancy, country road construction, and drinking water for people and livestock. The projects solved food and clothing problems for 26,000 farmers and herdsmen, and enabled 50,000 people to shake off poverty.

In 2005 Tibet started poverty-alleviation projects in ten selected townships, which are given three million yuan annually for this purpose. The object is to strengthen their infrastructure, develop industries with local features, and enhance the capabilities of the local poverty-stricken people. During the Tenth Five-Year Plan, the Tibet Regional Poverty Alleviation and Development Office arranged the allocation of poverty-alleviation and development funds totaling 1.518 billion yuan, and implemented 976 poverty-alleviation projects in various fields. These efforts shortened the region's poverty alleviation priority list from 1.48 million people to 373,000 people.

The net income of farmers and herdsmen maintained double-digit growth in the first three years of the 11th Five-Year Plan. On that basis, the government gave a total of 1.472 billion yuan for poverty alleviation to support 25,000 families and move 150,000 people into better houses. In 2006 the government carried out the project of providing houses for poverty-stricken families, and adopted measures such as comprehensively advancing poverty alleviation in townships and through developing industries, and providing training for labor transfer. This project, which proved very effective, laid a solid foundation for realizing the goals of the 11th Five-Year Plan. In 2007 the government allocated 193.044 million yuan to alleviate poverty. This provided new houses for 7,640 families, and established or improved training, job opportunities and employment services for farmers and herdsmen. Through various types of training, the region fulfilled the task of transferring 5,000 people to other employment in 2007 ahead of time. In the same year, more than 700,000 workers were employed outside the region, and earned a total of 950 million yuan. Meanwhile, 360 million yuan was invested for poverty-alleviation development. The first batch of development programs for poverty alleviation initiated by the Poverty Alleviation and Development Office of Tibet Autonomous Region in 2007 involved nine projects in nine villages and small towns, with a total input of 4.6124 million yuan, to resolve problems in people's livelihood and the development of the those villages and towns. Through the poverty-alleviation efforts, the per capita net income of farmers and herdsmen grew from 175 yuan in 1978 to 2,788 yuan in 2007, and continued to grow at a rate of over 10%. From 2008 to 2015 the region has earmarked 572.50 million yuan for the training of farmers and herdsmen, of which 16.65 million yuan will be spent annually on re-employment training for 350,000 workers in the farming and pastoral areas, so as to increase the number of people transferred to other fields by 10% annually. The regional government plans to transfer one million people out of farming and animal husbandry by the end of the 11th Five-Year Plan, and create an income of 1.8 billion yuan for them.

Although Tibet's poverty-alleviation work has scored great achievements, and the number of poverty-stricken people has dropped drastically, the task of poverty alleviation is still a heavy one. The remaining poverty-stricken population are scattered in different farming and pastoral areas with harsh natural conditions, low development levels, poor economic bases and high rates of falling back into poverty. This requires more funding, a higher level of poverty-alleviation development, and a combination of capital, projects and manpower, and needs to be conducted in concentrated periods of time. In 2008 the government of the Tibet Autonomous Region allocated a special fund of 172.26 million yuan for promoting poverty alleviation, invigorating border areas and helping the people prosper, innovating mechanisms, and facilitating poverty alleviation through economic development in all Tibetan villages. It believes that with a few more years of effort, the poverty-stricken population in Tibet will be greatly reduced.

50. What is the situation of Tibet's science and technology?

In the course of its modernization process, Tibet attaches great importance to the promotion and implementation of science and technology as well as scientific R&D. It has established a number of scientific research institutes, and brought in and fostered a group of personnel skilled in science and technology.

By the end of 2009 Tibet had established 33 scientific research institutes, among which 25 were independent and eight were affiliated to universities, government institutions or other organizations; 54 academic organizations of various kinds; 140 organizations at various levels for popularizing science and technology for agriculture and animal husbandry; and 48,524 scientific and technical personnel; over 74% of whom were Tibetans or people of other local ethnic minorities. There were also one state key laboratory, four science and technology demonstration zones of various kinds, five regional key laboratories, and three engineering technology research centers at the regional level. In addition, Tibet has set up a dozen science and technology demonstration bases characterized by farming and animal husbandry, including bases for fostering original crop seeds, improved vegetable varieties and semi-fine-wool sheep breeding, a comprehensive testing and demonstration base of cattle variety improvement, a base for planting and developing Tibetan Salvia miltiorrhiza (red sage root), a scientific demonstration base for the semi-artificial cultivation of wild rhizoma gastrodiae, and an industrial development base for fine-haired goat raising.

In 2009 Tibetan research specialists undertook 79 state scientific and technological projects and 67 key scientific and technological projects at the regional level, and one item of scientific and technological achievement above the provincial and ministry level. In addition, Tibet handled 195 patent applications, and 292 patents were granted. In the same year scientific research institutions in Tibet published 230 scientific papers, one of which was published abroad, and 24 titles of scientific works came off the press.

A number of basic or applied basic research institutes with particular features of the Qinghai-Tibet Plateau, such as Tibetan medicine R&D, energy R&D and application, and plateau meteorology and ecology were established and made new achievements. For instance, a series of basic research projects with regard to the plateau, including cosmic ray observation and deep exploration of the Qinghai-Tibet Plateau aroused deep interest both at home and abroad. Impressive progress was also made in the prevention and control of geological hazards such as mudrock flows, highway disasters and earthquakes, meteorology and the application of remote-sensing technology, integrated control of desertification and ecological environment protection, and the development and application of mineral resources. Some research findings even took the lead both at home and abroad. From 1978 to 2007 Tibet completed altogether 2,858 key scientific and technological projects at the state or regional level, of which 21 won national science and technology awards, and 704 won science and technology awards at the autonomous region level.

In 2009 Tibet introduced the "Golden Yak, Golden Sun Science and Technology Project" and other key scientific and technological programs, to further enhance the economy-supporting capacity of science and technology.

51. How is Tibet doing in energy development?

Tibet boasts abundant water, geothermal, wind and solar power. Statistics show that the natural water energy deposit in Tibet is 200 million kw, about 30% of the nation's total. The region has 354.8 billion cu m of surface water (13.5% of the nation's total) and 330 billion cu m of glacier water. The water energy deposit of the Yarlung Tsangpo River is over 80 million kw, and the total deposit reaches 90 million kw if its five major tributaries are included, namely the Dokshung Tsongpo, Nyangchu, Lhasa, Niyang and Yarlung rivers, with the total exploitable capacity being 110 million kw. Moreover, Tibet boasts the biggest geothermal energy reserve in China, with more than 600 geothermally active areas. It is also rich in solar energy, and the sunshine enjoyed by most places in Tibet every year is 3,100 to 3,400 hours, or an average of nine hours per day. Tibet is a particularly windy region. The wind speed is above three m per second on average for about 200 days every year, and the wind force in Nagchu and Ngari prefectures is above eight m per second in winter and spring. The regional government attaches great importance to energy development and utilization, and develops the aforesaid energy resources rationally and according to local circumstances, so as to benefit the local people.

Since its founding the Tibet Autonomous Region has built

many large- and medium-sized hydropower stations, including the Yardrok Yutso Lake Pumped Storage Power Station, Chalong Hydropower Station, Wokahe First-cascade Hydropower Station, Laman Hydro-Junction, and Purang Hydropower Station. During the Tenth Five-Year Plan Tibet started the construction of large-scale power stations, including those of Drigung and Shoka,[1] and made plans to build small-scale hydropower stations and upgrade the rural power grid. Since the beginning of the Tenth Five-Year Plan, the central government has invested a total of 2.898 billion yuan for rural hydropower construction, and built 79 power stations at the county level and 364 power stations at the township level. According to the Power Construction Plan for Regions without Electricity in the Tibet Autonomous Region, Tibet will build 60 standard hydropower stations and 698 small hydropower stations[2] in farming and pastoral areas not covered by the electricity grid, so as to provide electricity to more people. During the 11th Five-Year Plan Tibet will protect and develop the water resources of major rivers such as the Yarlung Tsangpo, Lancangjiang, Nujiang, Jinshajiang, Lhasa, Nyangchu and Niyang rivers. In May 2007 construction of the Laohuzui Power Station started, which will have an installed capacity of 102,000 kw. According to the 11th Five-Year Plan for Tibet's Electricity Development and the Goal for 2020, Tibet will start to build a 220-v main power grid in 2010, and the whole region's total installed capacity will be 1.2 million kw.

By that year Tibet will have solved the electricity problem for most of the region's farmers and herdsmen, and 90% of the region's population, or all villages and townships, will have access to electricity.

Research into and development of solar power started early in Tibet. In the mid-1960s the Tibet Architecture Design Institute developed solar water heaters. In 1986 the "comprehensive solar energy development and utilization program of Tibet" was listed in the region's "Spark Plan." In recent years Tibet has carried out the "Sunbeam Plan," "Light of Science Program" and "Solar Power Program of Ngari Prefecture" to solve rural electricity problems through promoting solar power generation. In 2002 the State Planning Commission poured 810 million yuan into the "Bringing Electricity to the Countryside" program, and built photovoltaic power stations for 300 villages. Thanks to Ngari Prefecture's solar power program, which was concluded in 2005, 70,000 people in that prefecture, renowned as the "roof of the world's roof," now benefit from electricity for the first time. Tibet utilizes solar power as a kind of green energy and promotes it as an industry with local features. Its next step is to industrialize solar power generation and turn this resource advantage into an economic advantage. By 2006 Tibet had built 400 photovoltaic power stations, including seven solar power stations with generating capacities of between 10 kw to 100 kw. The region's total installed capacity of solar power stations reached 9,000 kw, enough to satisfy 200,000 people's need for electricity, and the region also promoted the installation of 150,000 solar cookers and built 200,000 sq m solar collectors for room and water heating. Through utilizing solar energy, Tibet has finally solved the electricity problem for places in which county governments are seated and compacted areas inhabited by local residents, and 650,000 farmers and herdsmen have bidden farewell to life without electricity. With the completion of high-power solar photovoltaic power stations, Tibet ranks first in China in terms of solar power utilization scale and rate.

Tibet is one of China's most geothermally active regions. There are currently more than 600 known geothermally active areas, with a potential power-generating capacity of 800,000 kw. In November 1981 the Yangbajing geothermal power station installed its first 3,000-kw generator. By 1989 its installed capacity reached 19,000 kw greatly easing Lhasa's electricity shortage.

Tibet has a special advantage in wind power. By November 1987 a total of 380 wind-power generators had been installed in Nagchu Prefecture alone, providing electricity to herdsmen who had relied on butter lamps for generations previously.

Before 1951 electricity was almost unknown in Tibet. Farmers and herdsmen used pine-oil or butter lamps for illumination, and burnt cow dung and grass to keep themselves warm. After Tibet's liberation in 1951 Tibet's power industry started virtually from scratch, but developed rapidly. Now, with a total installed capacity of 720,000 kw, the region's annual power generation stands at 1.8 billion kwh. The region's cities and counties are now ablaze with lights at night, and the people of Tibet now enjoy all the conveniences brought by electricity, such as air-conditioners, refrigerators, color television sets, electric tea machines, computers and other modern household appliances.

Electricity provides powerful energy support for the socio-economic development of Tibet. From 2001 to 2009 the generation level of the Tibet Electric Power Company grew from 734 million kwh to 1.8 billion kwh; the total length of transmission lines with voltage above 35 kv increased 1.39 times, from 2,206 km to 5,265 km; and the capacity of main substations increased 3.66 times, from 329,900 kva to 1.5367 million kva. The development of the power industry has played a significant role in promoting Tibet's socio-economic development and improving the people's living standard.

By the end of 2009 the population with access to electricity was 2.1 million. In the same year more than 73% of the population had access to electricity, and electricity coverage reached 100% in places where county and township governments were located, and 60% in large villages. Wider electricity coverage has greatly improved the people's material and cultural lives, and enabled farmers and herdsmen to enjoy the fruits of modern civilization.

Tibet also has abundant water resources, with latent deposits of 210 million kw and exploitable deposits of 140 million kw, both figures ranking first in China. More efforts should be made to explore water resources, because only 0.4% of the exploitable deposits are in use. However, common practices such as building large- and medium-scale power stations and transmitting electricity through the grid cannot solve the problems in all areas without electricity, because of Tibet's vast area, complex geological and meteorological conditions, sparsely scattered population and low demand for electricity in many areas. Therefore, making full use of renewable resources such as the region's rich solar, wind and geothermal power sources, and small hydropower stations as well as conventional power stations is the key to solving Tibet's electricity problem.

After the Fifth Tibet Work Symposium in 2010, the State Grid put forward measures to support Tibet's power development. In the next phase of development, Tibet's power development will be planned scientifically while allowing moderate advancement ahead of the plan. The region will vigorously develop hydropower, actively utilize new energy resources in accordance with local conditions and develop multiple energy resources. The region will also accelerate grid construction and network connection, and improve the safety, stability, reliability and economic efficiency of the grid. Attention will also be paid to energy conservancy, energy development, management, construction, and efficiency as well as quality, so as to realize the even-more-rapid development of Tibet's power industry.

Tibet started to promote large-scale utilization of methane in 2006. In 2009 Tibet earmarked 158 million yuan in a project to construct facilities using methane to replace traditional firewood. Under the project, Tibet constructed methane tanks for 114,000 families, and distributed solar cookers to 395,000 families in rural areas. According to the Rural Methane Construction Plan for the 11th Five-Year Plan of the Tibet Autonomous Region, Tibet will build methane tanks for 200,000 families in 59 selected counties by the end of the 11th Five-Year Plan[3]. By the end of the 12th Five-Year Plan methane is expected to be universal in Tibet's rural areas.

The widespread utilization of clean energy resources has greatly reduced the use of cow dung, firewood and grass as fuel, curbs grassland deterioration, protects the ecological environment and improves the living standard of the region's farmers and herdsmen.

Notes:

[1] According *Tibet Daily*'s report on September 27, 2008, the first 10,000 kw generator of Shoka Hydropower Station started operation on September 24, 2008. The station has installed four 10,000 kw generators, with an annual electricity generation of 182 million kwh.

[2] See *Tibet Daily*, October 10, 2008 (front page)

[3] This project alone will reduce the expenditure of farmers and herdsmen by 200 million yuan. See *Tibet Daily*, September 24, 2008 (front page).

52. When did Tibet's modern industry start? Does Tibet have high-tech enterprises?

Before its peaceful liberation in 1951 Tibet had a very weak industrial basis. Industry in Tibet consisted of only a 125-kw small hydropower station built around 1931, a small mint and a small machinery factory. Owing to poor management and a shortage of auxiliary equipment, the hydropower station which supplied electricity only to the handful of senior officials and aristocrats had to close shortly after going into operation. At that time Tibet had only 120 people working in industry, making for a negligible industrial scale and output.

Since the Democratic Reform in 1959, with the support of the central government, Tibet established its own modern industrial enterprises, from scratch to a certain scale and later growing into a major force in the region's economic development. Currently, Tibet has a modern industrial system of over 20 sectors with distinctive local features, including energy, light industry, textiles, machinery, timber, mining, building materials, chemicals, pharmaceuticals, printing, and food processing.

Continual improvements in Tibet's industrial system are strongly promoting secondary industry and the region's economy as a whole. Tibet has formed a system consisting of new types of energy resources, with hydropower as the backbone, supplemented by other energy resources such as geothermal, wind and solar power.

In 2009 Tibet speeded up its industrial construction, obtained national discount loans for industrial revitalization and investment subsidies totaling 110 million yuan, and strongly supported the development of industries with regional features.

Tibet's industrial output steadily increased, with the output of major industrial products rising rapidly. The output of electricity, cement, beer and bottled (canned) drinking water in 2009 rose by 10.6%, 13.1%, 13.7% and 101.8%, respectively, over the previous year.

In 2009 the added value of overall industry in Tibet reached 3.267 billion yuan, up 12.9% over 2008. Of this, the added value of the industrial enterprises above the designated size[1] reached 2.756 billion yuan, up 10.8%. The added value of light industry was 1.1 billion yuan, up 16.4%, and that of heavy industry 1.656 billion yuan, an increase of 7.8%. The added value of state-owned and state-controlled enterprises together amounted to 1.369 billion yuan, up 12.2%. With regard to registered type, the added value of state-owned enterprises reached 963 million yuan, a rise of 2.5%; that of collective enterprises 65 million yuan, a fall of 4.9%; that of joint-stock enterprises 1.161 billion yuan, up 15.2%; that of cooperative enterprises with shares held by employees 5 million yuan, a decrease of 60.9%; that of enterprises run by foreigners and people from Hong Kong, Macao and Taiwan 403 million yuan, up 34.0%; and that of other ownership enterprises 159 million yuan, up 1.7%.

The profits of the industrial enterprises above the designated size reached 563 million yuan, up 4.9% over 2008. The profit of state-owned and state-controlled enterprises was 107 million yuan, an increase of 7.6 times; that of collective enterprises 22 million yuan, a rise of 50.3%; and that of joint-stock enterprises 368 million yuan, a fall of 6.8%. As for the industrial enterprises above the designated size, their ratio of sales to gross output value reached 97.2%.

In 2009 the output of cement reached 1.8765 million tons, a rise of 14.9% over 2008; that of generated energy 1.8 billion kwh, up 12.5%; that of beer 113,000 tons, a rise of 25.0%; that of prepared Chinese medicine (Tibetan medicine and pharmacology) 1,319 tons, up 5.4%; that of water supply 10,873 tons, up 17.5%; and that of bottled (canned) drinking water 65,800 tons, up 71.0%; that of chrome ore 112,300 tons, up 6.0%.

Tibet attaches great importance to the development of high-tech enterprises in its modernization process. In recent years Tibet has used high and new technologies to develop resources with local features to manufacture a wide range of high-tech products with market competitiveness. By 2002 there were 15 high-tech enterprises in Tibet, with a total added value of over 800 million yuan. Tibetan high-tech enterprises have developed dozens of high-tech products in 12 categories including medicines and pharmaceuticals, energy, chemicals and telecommunications. Many Tibetan medicines, such as Cheezheng Pain Relieving Plaster and Nuodingkang (or Rhodiola) Capsules have entered the US, Korean and Japanese markets. In May 2006 the High-Tech Enterprises Evaluation Committee of the Tibet Autonomous Region reexamined old high-tech enterprises, and approved seven new enterprises. At present, Tibet has 21 high-tech enterprises, and won 34 progress prizes in science and technology in 2006 and 2007.

Note:

[1] Here the industrial enterprise above the designated size refers to any state-owned enterprise or any private enterprise whose annual revenue has reached 5 million yuan or more.

53. How is Tibet doing in highway construction? How do the highways influence Tibet's economic buildup and people's livelihood?

From 2001 to 2005 Tibet completed road construction projects at a total cost of 14.692 billion yuan, and renovated roads totaling 2,000 km, including the Qinghai-Tibet Highway, Sichuan-Tibet Highway and China-Nepal Highway.

In 2009 Tibet completed highway construction projects at a total cost of 6.062 billion yuan, registering a growth rate of 34.65% compared with 2008. The total highway mileage had reached 53,845 km by the end of 2009, 2,531 km more than that in 2008. Length of paved roads reached 3,279 km, 384 km more than in 2008. Now 67% of the counties in Tibet have asphalt roads, 97.95% of the townships and 80.25% of large villages are linked by highways.

In 2009 China scaled up highway construction in Tibet. The number of projects, total funds, number of people benefited and effect on economic development were all unprecedented. According to official statistics, road construction contributed 1.2 percentage points to Tibet's economic growth rate, or 9.6% of the growth. In the same year Tibet started 19 key highway construction projects, including the highway that would connect Lhasa and Gongkar Airport, and National Highway G214

(Chamdo-Pangda Airport section), and completed and put into use 11 projects, including National Highway G317 (Jomda-Thopa section) and National Highway G219 (Montser-Barga section). Also in the same year Tibet started 95 rural highway connection projects with a total funding of 780 million yuan, and a total mileage of 4,081 km, to link 19 townships and 213 large villages.

At present Tibet's road network has formed the pattern of "three longitudes and three latitudes" with Lhasa as the center. The network connects Tibet with Sichuan and Yunnan in the east, Xinjiang Uygur Autonomous Region in the northwest and Qinghai in the north, and crosses the border to connect China with India and Nepal. At present, Tibet has basically completed its road network, featuring provincial highway linkage, and connection between prefecture-level cities, counties and townships, upgraded highway technological standards, and greatly improved the road conditions.

The advanced road network is helping more and more farmers and herdsmen to leave the remote mountains and isolated grasslands, become integrated into the market economy and become better-off.

54. How was the Qinghai-Tibet Railway constructed? How has the railway changed the local people's life? How does it influence Tibet's economy?

The building of a railway between Qinghai and Tibet had been the Tibetan's people's aspiration for many years. The CPC Central Committee and the State Council made the strategic decision of constructing the Qinghai-Tibet Railway at the turn of the century, and listed it among the landmark projects for the development of the western regions. Its completion and operation were highly significant for the two places' socio-economic development, ethnic unity, and the improvement of the people's livelihood.

The 1,956-km railway begins in Xining, capital of Qinghai Province, and ends in Lhasa, capital of the Tibet Autonomous Region. It is the longest and highest plateau railway in the world. The first section of the railway, from Xining to Golmud, was built in 1979, and opened to traffic in 1984. The second section, 1,142 km from Golmud to Lhasa, was formally started on June 29, 2001, at a total cost of more than 26.2 billion yuan from the central government. To construct the railway, the engineers had to overcome extremely severe challenges in railway construction – perennially frozen ground, high altitudes, frigid temperatures, lack of oxygen, and protection of the unique, fragile ecological environment of the Tibet plateau. The successful trial run of the

Qinghai-Tibet Railway on July 1, 2006 ended Tibet's history of being without railways. The advent of the railway has greatly accelerated the circulation of people, materials, capital and information, and has a great and direct boosting effect on the economic development of Qinghai and Tibet, especially on regions along the railway line. Among the changes brought about by the Qinghai-Tibet Railway, the most distinctive one is the growing demand for tourism. According to statistics from the Tourism Bureau of the Tibet Autonomous Region, in the five months from the going into operation of the Qinghai-Tibet Railway to the end of 2006, Tibet received 1.86 million tourists from both at home and abroad, an increase of 48% over the same period of the previous year. The number of visits to Tibet that year was 2.51 million, up 39.5% over the previous year. From July to September, 2006 the occupancy rate of hotels in Lhasa was above 95%. It was very hard to get a ticket for the Potala Palace, and what was even harder to get was a train ticket for entering or leaving Tibet. The tourism revenue in 2006 increased from 1.93 billion yuan to 2.771 billion yuan, up 43.6% over the figure for 2005. The added value of tertiary industry, driven by tourism, reached 16.28 billion yuan, an increase of 11.8% over the previous year. Residents along the railway all benefited from the economic growth. By the end of July 2008 the Qinghai-Tibet Railway had handled 5.56 million passengers and 4.05 million tons of cargo.

The completion and operation of the Qinghai-Tibet Railway

has optimized Tibet's economic growth structure, rationalized its industrial structure, and increased the proportion of its secondary and tertiary industries by one and 1.5 percentage points, respectively, thereby greatly accelerating economic growth in Tibet. In particular, it has attracted more investors to the region. Foreign exchange earnings from tourism reached US$78.73 million in 2006, an increase of 1.5 times over the previous year, among which the foreign exchange earnings from the operation of the railway to the end of December reached US$41.66 million. In addition, the operation of the railway promoted the development of and investment in the non-public economy. During the economic and commercial talks at the traditional Tibetan Shoton Festival in 2006, a total of 56 contracts were signed, with the aggregate investment totaling 3.17 billion yuan. The number of the self-employed and private enterprises increased by 7,500 in 2006, the biggest increase in recent years, to bring the total number of registered self-employed and private enterprises to 77,900 by the end of June 2008.[1]

The completion and operation of the Qinghai-Tibet Railway has broadened the minds of the Tibetan people, who are now eager to see the world outside. The railway also facilitates Tibet's exchanges with other places, and enhances ethnic unity by benefiting people of all ethnic groups.

Note:

[1] See *Tibet Daily*, August 30, 2008 (front page).

55. What special measures has the government of Tibet Autonomous Region taken to train Tibetan technical and managerial personnel?

With the deepening of reform and opening-up, especially after the implementation of the national strategy of developing the western regions, the shortage of technical and managerial personnel in Tibet was found to restrict Tibet's rapid economic development. To solve the problem, the central government and the government of the Tibet Autonomous Region adopted various measures. While increasing the number of inland technical and managerial personnel assigned to Tibet so as to pass on experience to the local personnel, they have also intensified the training of Tibetan technical personnel by ministries and commissions under the State Council, and universities; secondment to posts in relevant departments of inland provinces; and training and further education abroad. At present, a dozen colleges and universities in China provide training for technical and managerial personnel for Tibet. For instance, Renmin University of China, Hunan Agricultural University and Tibet University constantly hold medium- and long-term technical training courses and classes for postgraduates. In 2002 alone, 7,215 ethnic-minority cadres, a large proportion of whom were Tibetans, received training at these colleges and universities.

Among them, 141 ethnic-minority people, mainly Tibetans, were sent to nine countries and regions for special technical training, including the United States, Israel, Canada, the Netherlands, Germany and New Zealand. This is still in practice now and will continue in future. Personnel having received such training are playing positive roles at their posts.

56. What is the situation of Tibet's border trade with India and Nepal?

To date, the Tibet Autonomous Region has opened 28 border trade markets with India and Nepal. Dram and Purang have become China's window to South Asia. China and India formally resumed trade in 1992 in Tibet's Purang and Kungri in India's Uttar Pradesh Province, and opened another pair of border trade markets in Tibet's Juparand and India's Namgia in Himachal Pradesh. After Chinese Premier Zhu Rongji's visit to India in January 2002, agreements were reached in many aspects between China and India. In 2006 the two sides decided to open the Yadong trade port every year from July 1 to October 31. On July 6, 2006, in Natho La, Yadong, an opening ceremony was held to formally open Yadong port and resume the Natho La trade market. In 2007 relevant departments of the two countries agreed to prolong the opening from four months to six, i.e., from May 1 to October 31. With the completion and operation of the Qinghai-Tibet Railway, the cost of border trade between China and India was reduced, and the prospects for bilateral trade and cooperation have improved. Tibet's foreign trade import and export reached US$393 million-worth, an increase of 19.8% over 2006 and an all-time high since 1995. According to statistics from the Lhasa customs, from July 1, 2006 to April 30, 2007 the number of inbound and outbound passengers at the Dram port and Lhasa Airport was 37,566, among whom 14,578 were inbound and 22,988 were outbound. This resulted in a surge of import and export of tourism commodities. In the same period Tibet imported fragrant incense worth US$320,000, woodcarvings worth US$40,000, medicines worth US$80,000 and jewelry worth US$30,000 from Nepal. It exported garments made of synthetic fiber worth US$36.46 million, apples worth US$9.31 million, garlic worth US$1.91 million and electric cookers worth US$1.01 million to Nepal. The trade volume with India at Yadong port reached RMB2.67 million yuan from May to August 2008, 2.43 times the figure of the previous year.[1]

Note:

[1] See "Expanding Opening-up in Tibet's Border Areas" in *Tibet Daily*, September 27, 2008 (page 6).

57. As Tibet's development and construction needs substantial labor, will there be growing immigration into the region?

Tibet's development and construction need a large quantity of high-quality labor, especially specialized personnel. However, due to the shortage of local skilled people, Tibet has to introduce a substantial amount of labor, specialized technical personnel in particular. Normally, these workers will return to their native places after the projects are completed. This is a normal and rational population flow in the market economy and is totally different from population immigration. In completing projects, the Tibet Autonomous Region prefers to use local labor first, so as to increase employment for farmers and herdsmen. In fact, the construction of major projects in Tibet uses locals as the main body of the labor force. Therefore, there is no problem of immigration in Tibet for its development and construction.

The total population of Tibet was about 1.852767 million in 1980, among whom Tibetans accounted for 1.718238 million and Han people accounted for 122,356, making up 92.74% and 6.6%, respectively. Statistics from 2009 show that Tibetans and other ethnic minorities accounted for about 95% of Tibet's population. This shows that in the past 30 years the proportion of Tibetans and other local people in the total Tibetan population increased rather than dropped. The population structure experienced no fundamental changes in these decades, and the Tibetans still form the majority of the population of Tibet. Most Han and people of other ethnic groups from outside working in Tibet are specialized personnel or technicians with high education and special skills. They are from every corner of China. Overcoming various difficulties, such as high altitude sickness, they make great contributions to Tibet's economic, social and cultural development together with the Tibetan people. Population movements among regions are normal in every country. It is also part of basic human rights.

58. What is the size of unemployment in Tibet? What policies and measures has China taken to increase employment there?

The government of the Tibet Autonomous Region attaches great importance to the issue of unemployment, and has launched a series of preferential measures to vigorously promote employment. The first is to promote employment and reemployment through such preferential policies as reducing fees and taxes, and extending small loans. The second is to create job opportunities by developing industries with regional features such as tourism, Tibetan medicine and ethnic crafts. The third is to intensify employment and reemployment training, and provide vocational guidance and introduction services. The fourth is to create more jobs in non-profit undertakings funded by the government. By March 2010 the number of urban unemployed in Tibet was 20,000, with the overall unemployment rate kept under 4.3%.

59. What is China's attitude toward aid projects launched by foreign NGOs in Tibet?

At present, non-governmental organizations (NGOs) from nearly 20 countries have launched more than 100 aid projects in Tibet free of charge. Most projects supplement the socio-economic development of the Tibet Autonomous Region, and their experience is worth learning from.

The development of all undertakings in Tibet would have been impossible without support from the central government and other provinces. It is also necessary for Tibet to cooperate with various international institutions and organizations and learn from their good practices, especially successful experience in certain fields. Tibet will continue to adhere to the policy of reform and opening-up, and sincerely welcome institutions and organizations from every corner of the world to make investments and launch cooperation projects in Tibet.

60. Has Tibet established a foreign trade system compatible with international norms?

In its opening-up endeavors the Chinese government has taken a series of preferential policies and measures to invigorate Tibet's economy and speed up its economic construction. For instance, Tibet can retain all the foreign exchange it earns from overseas trade and sell imported products in the hinterland. Recently, the government of the Tibet Autonomous Region decided to set up foreign economic and technological development zones in accordance with the state policy on opening wider to the outside world, increase the number of open border ports, allow foreign business people to lease land, and expand border trade with neighboring countries as well as entrepot trade.

Tibet now has four first-class ports approved by the government (land ports Dram, Gyirong and Purang, and Lhasa Airport) and one second-class port (Riwo). It has 28 traditional border free markets and four formal trading ports. Dram, Purang and other important ports, as ports with expanding influence on neighboring regions, have become China's window to South Asia.

61. What is Tibet's tourism situation? How are its tourism resources being tapped?

Tourism is a strategic pillar industry in Tibet, and enjoys development priority. Tibet's attractive natural scenery and local customs make the region one of the most popular destinations for visitors from all over the world. Tibet's transportation, which has been greatly improved since the Qinghai-Tibet Railway was opened to traffic, provides good conditions for the development of its tourism.

From 1980 to 2009 the accumulated tourism revenue in the region reached 24.497 billion yuan. The revenue of 2006 after the completion and operation of the Qinghai-Tibet Railway was 2.77 billion yuan, taking up 9.6% of the region's GDP. The total tourism revenue in 2007 increased to 4.85 billion yuan, taking up 14.2% of the region's GDP. However, the March 14 Incident and the global financial crisis in 2008 affected Tibet's tourism. That year Tibet received 2.25 million visitors, and realized 2.259 billion yuan in tourism revenue. In 2009 the number of tourists was 5.61 million, and the revenue was 5.599 billion yuan, 39.20% and 15.4% higher than in the same period of 2007, respectively. Tourism has become an important pillar industry for Tibet's socio-economic development.

By 2009 there were 1,351 tourism enterprises in Tibet, and

28,400 people were directly involved in the industry and more than 172,100 people indirectly involved, among whom Tibetan made up 62.8%. It is worth mentioning that 10,460 households, involving 41,844 farmers and herdsmen, are now engaged in the tourism industry, and the revenue in this regard has reached 255.96 million yuan, with the increased per capita revenue reaching 6,116 yuan.

Developing more scenic spots, enlivening the local economy and allowing the local residents to prosper are the ways to accelerate Tibet's economic development and increase the incomes of farmers and herdsmen.

The Fifth Tibet Work Symposium further defined the strategic role of tourism in Tibet's economic development, and proposed the building of Tibet into an important world tourist destination, and to transform its resource advantages into economic ones. To this end, we must, on the one hand, intensify publicity to promote Tibet as an important international tourist destination, and, on the other, accelerate tourism infrastructure construction, at the same time launching in an all-round way the 12th Five-Year Plan infrastructure projects on the basis of our achievements during the 11th Five-Year Plan, so as to foster a fine tourism environment.

62. What procedures do foreigners have to undergo to visit Tibet? What are those for foreign journalists?

Owing to its tough natural conditions characterized by high altitude, cold climate and thin air as well as its backward transportation, Tibet's capacity for tourist reception is limited. To guarantee the success of tours and tourists' safety, before entering Tibet foreigners must apply to Chinese embassies, consulates or overseas offices of Tibetan travel agencies, get approval from Tibetan tourism administration department and finally get an entry visa issued by a Chinese embassy or consulate. However, with the constant economic development in Tibet, its tourism is also gaining speed. At the end of 2002, to meet the trend of the increase in the number of tourists to Tibet, the Chinese government accelerated Tibet's opening up, issued new regulations on foreign visitors and lifted restrictions that foreign visitors must form a group of at least five people to visit Tibet. So individual travelers can also enter Tibet now. The number of tourists from both at home and abroad to Tibet in 2006, when the Qinghai-Tibet Railway was opened to traffic, was 2.51 million, 4.02 million in 2007 and 5.61 million in 2009. Every year more than 100,000 foreign tourists visit Tibet, and the number reached 174,900 in 2009. Tibet is expecting more foreign visitors as the region becomes more open and its tourism facilities improve. However, it is better for foreign visitors to travel in Tibet in group in order to make the travel more smooth and safer.

Foreign journalists are welcome to cover the Tibet Autonomous Region, and we are ready to provide all necessary assistance. In recent years we have received many foreign journalists from different parts of the world and helped them with their interviews. Due to Tibet's special geographical, climatic and environmental conditions as well as poor transportation conditions, foreign journalists should also follow the same rules and regulations as other foreign visitors. The Tibet Autonomous Region will take further measures to improve its work efficiency and quality of service in this regard.

63. Have Tibetan guides been eliminated in the Tibet Autonomous Region?

Each year before the tourism season guides are trained for Tibet. Only those qualified can go to their posts, and those found incompetent professionally are disqualified. They are from the Tibetan, Han and other ethnic groups.

To ease the shortage of guides in Tibet, the National Tourism Administration of the People's Republic of China has been selecting outstanding guides from major inland travel agencies for Tibet since 2003. After arriving in Tibet they are twinned with local guides to improve the latter's professional skills as well as their own. Besides, the National Tourism Administration supports Sichuan University and Zhejiang University in enrolling altogether 80 students majoring in tourism every year as high-level personnel for Tibetan tourism.

Meanwhile, tourism departments at various levels in Tibet fathom their own potential and establish tourism training centers to train guides and related staff annually. Over the past five years more than 5,000 such personnel have been trained, and so the shortage of guides in Tibet during the tourism season has been greatly alleviated.

Religious Beliefs VI

64. Do all the people of Tibet follow Tibetan Buddhism? What are the features of Tibetan Buddhism?

Most Tibetan religious believers in Tibet practice Tibetan Buddhism. Tibet's native Bon religion still has certain influence in some areas, and there are small numbers of Tibetans believing in Islam and Catholicism.

Before Buddhism was introduced to Tibet in the seventh century, during the reign of the Tubo king Songtsen Gampo, the native Bon religion was prevalent. Songtsen Gampo's two wives – the Chinese Princess Wencheng of the Tang Dynasty and the Nepali Princess Tritsun – both believed in Buddhism, and with their support Buddhism rapidly spread in Tibet. Over time, Buddhism in Tibet absorbed some elements of Bon, including certain deities and sacrificial rituals. Tibetan Buddhism is marked by the presence of Living Buddhas, reincarnated senior lamas.

In the mid-ninth century, King Gldarma tried to stamp out Buddhism, and many believers fled central Tibet. Buddhism was almost destroyed in the central Ü-Tsang region until several decades later, when the exiles returned and resumed the preaching of Buddhist teachings. So the history of Tibetan Buddhism contains the Early Propagation and Later Propagation periods, with Gldarma's persecution of Buddhism as the watershed. The returnees sought the patronage of various political figures, and

as a result divergences in Buddhist teachings and related interpretations and differences in garb appeared, leading to the emer-
gence of a number of sects, which later became four major ones:
Nyingma, Kagyu, Sakya and Gelug, commonly known as the
red, white, striped and yellow sects, respectively.

Nyingma Sect, founded in the 11th-12th centuries, is the
oldest sect of Tibetan Buddhism. The word "Nyingma" means
"ancient" or "old" in the Tibetan language. The Nyingma tradition traces its origin to the Indian master Padmasambhava (The
Lotus-born), who preached Buddhism in Tibet in the eighth
century. Nyingma sect chiefly propagates ancient translations of
esoteric texts, so it is often referred to as the "old sect." Due to
its relatively loose organizational structure and lack of unified
teaching, the Nyingma tradition has never had a monastery of
centralized authority or a unified, powerful monastic segment.
As a result, its influence was smaller compared to other sects in
Tibetan region.

Kagyu Sect, founded in the early 11th century, traces its
origin to Marpa and Milarepa. Because masters like Marpa and
Milarepa worn white monk robes when practicing Buddhism, it
is also known as the "white sect." In its early years, the Kagyu
tradition had two lineages, Shangpa and Dakpo. The Dakpo Kagyu was founded by Dakpo Lhaje, a disciple of Milarepa. The
four major disciples of Dakpo Lhaje established their own monasteries and had their followers, forming the Phagdru, Tsalpa,

Barom and Karma lineages, respectively. The Phagdru tradition further developed into eight lineages: Drigung, Taklung, Drukpa, Yazang, Trophu, Shugseb, Yerpa and Martsang. The lineages of the Dakpo Kagyu were later referred to as the "four great and eight lesser" schools. The leading masters of the Phagdru Kagyu School received titles from the central governments of China's Yuan (1271-1368) and Ming (1368-1644) dynasties, and formed in Tibet a local government historically known as the Phadgru government. After the Gelug Sect took over political power in the Qing Dynasty (1644-1911), the Kagyu Sect's influence gradually declined. Today's reincarnation system of Tibetan Buddhism originated in the Kagyu tradition.

Sakya Sect was founded by Khon Konchok Gyalpo in the 11th century. The name Sakya was derived from the location of the tradition's first monastery, a place called Sakya in Tsang River valley in Back Tibet. The monastery, built in 1073, is commonly known as the "striped sect" for its striped walls of dark red, white and grey, symbolizing Manjushri (the bodhisattva of wisdom), Kuanyin (the bodhisattva of mercy), and Vajradhara (the bodhisattva of energy and power), respectively. For a time in the Yuan Dynasty, the Sakya Sect was supported by the central government. Phagpa, one of the five patriarchs of the tradition, was appointed by the Yuan's founding emperor Kublai Khan as an imperial spiritual advisor and head of the Zongzhi Yuan (later renamed Xuanzheng Yuan or Ministry of Tibetan Governance), in charge of Buddhist and Tibetan affairs across the country. With the support from the central government of the Yuan empire, the Sakya Sect established its theocratic rule, historically known as the Sakya regime, in Tibet. Following the collapse of the Yuan empire, the Sakya regime was replaced by the Phadgru regime of the Kagyu Sect.

Gelug Sect, founded by Tsongkhapa in the 15th century, is the youngest of the major sects of Tibetan Buddhism. The Gelug tradition stresses strict monastic discipline among lamas, and advocates the equal importance of the tranquility of the mind and insight into truth for delivering all living beings from world sufferings. The name Gelug means "virtuous order" in the Tibetan language, so the tradition is also called the Sect of Virtuous Order. It is commonly known as the "yellow sect" because the lamas wear yellow monk robes and hats. The Gelug Sect was founded at a time when the Sakya and Kagyu sects were contending for power in Tibet. At that time, the upper-class lamas neglected the commandments and lived a decadent life; political corruption was common and social dissatisfaction prevailed. The Gelug Sect won the support of the local chieftains and the public for its strict monastic discipline, and soon grew into a social force with wide influence. The Monlam Festival (Great Prayer Meeting) initiated by Tsongkhapa in Lhasa in 1409 officially marked the founding of the Gelug Sect. Then the master established the Gandain Monastery, the first monastery of this tradition. Among Tsongkhapa's disciples were the successive incarnations of the Dalai and Panchen Living Buddhas. In 1653 the Fifth Dalai Lama went to Beijing and was received by the Qing emperor. He was then granted an honorific title and put in charge of Buddhist affairs nationwide. In the mid-18th century, the Qing central government placed the Tibetan local government into the hands of the Seventh Dalai Lama. From that time, the Gelug Sect was the ruling religious and political power in Tibet until the central government of the People's Republic of China announced the dismissal of the local government of Tibet on March 28, 1959.

65. What is China's religious policy? Is freedom of religious belief fully protected and respected in Tibet?

Respecting and protecting citizens' freedom of religious belief, a long-term basic state policy of China, is fully guaranteed by law.

Article 36 of the Constitution of the People's Republic of China stipulates, "Citizens of the People's Republic of China enjoy freedom of religious belief. No state organ, public organization or individual may compel citizens to believe in, or not to believe in, any religion; nor may they discriminate against citizens who believe in, or do not believe in, any religion. The state protects normal religious activities. No one may make use of religion to engage in activities that disrupt public order, impair the health of citizens or interfere with the educational system of the state. Religious bodies and religious affairs may not be subject to any form of foreign domination."

In addition to the Constitution, the Law on Regional Ethnic Autonomy, Criminal Law, General Principles of the Civic Law, and other laws also contain stipulations on the protection of citizens' freedom of religious belief, forbidding discrimination against citizens on the grounds of them having or not having religious belief.

The Tibet Autonomous Region is home to several religions,

including Tibetan Buddhism, Islam and Catholicism. Stipulations on the protection of citizens' freedom of religious belief in China's Constitution and other laws are earnestly implemented in Tibet. Religious believers in Tibet are protected by the Constitution and other laws, and fully enjoy the freedom of conducting normal religious activities.

Today, there are over 1,700 sites for Tibetan Buddhist activities and over 46,000 Buddhist monks and nuns in Tibet. Prayer niches and shrines to the Buddha can be found in the homes of almost all religious believers. It is estimated that more than one million Buddhists go on pilgrimage to Lhasa and offer incense to Buddha each year. Prayer banners and mounds of *mani* stones inscribed with "six-syllable mantra," believers devoutly prostrating themselves on the ground, spinning prayer wheels or on pilgrimages, can be seen everywhere in Tibet. Religious believers and patriotic Buddhist monks and nuns show support for and satisfaction with the state's current religious policies.

The local government of the Tibet Autonomous Region implements the policy of separating religion from politics, and exercises its administration over religious activities and organizations in Tibet in accordance with the law. It makes efforts to ensure that no religious organizations or believers engage in activities that undermine national unity and disrupt public order, and that monasteries do not interfere in administrative, judicial, educational and social management activities. The local government of Tibet also encourages and supports the efforts of religious circles to provide interpretations of religious disciplines and doctrines that are in line with the progress of the times, and guides Tibetan Buddhism to adapt to the socialist system.

Reference:

1. Since the 1980s, the central government has allocated funds of a total of 700 million yuan and enormous amounts of gold and silver for the maintenance, restoration and protection of monasteries in Tibet.

2. A large number of Tibetan Buddhist books, such as the *Tengyur* and *Kangyur* of the Tibetan *Tripitaka*, have been collated and published.

3. Over 40 traditional religious festivals, including the Sakadawa Festival commemorating the anniversary of the birth of the Buddha, have been reinstated.

4. The title *Lharam Geshe*, the highest degree in the monastic education system of the Gelug Sect, has been restored.

5. The Tibet branch of the Buddhist Association of China and the sub-branch Buddhist associations in seven autonomous prefectures and cities in Tibet have been established.

66. How does the Tibet Autonomous Region handle the relations between politics and religious beliefs? Can a Communist Party member, for example, follow any religion?

China follows the principle of separating religion from politics and education. This principle covers the following three aspects: First, the state respects freedom of religious belief, protects normal religious activities and safeguards the lawful rights and interests of religious circles; second, the state treats all religions equally, and no one may make use of the state's political power to support or suppress any religion; and third, religions should conduct their activities within the sphere prescribed by law, and their activities should not disrupt public order or interfere with the administrative, judicial and educational systems of the state. In conclusion, harmonious administration can be achieved as long as religious activities are carried out within the sphere of the Constitution and other laws of the state.

China's Constitution stipulates that citizens have the freedom to believe in, or not to believe in, any religion. As materialists, Communist Party members do not believe in any religion. In accordance with the CPC Constitution, Party members are atheists, and thus should not follow any religion. Those who officially withdraw from the Party have freedom of religious belief.

67. What is the reincarnation system for living Buddha in Tibetan Buddhism? When were the practice established by China's central government to grant the honorific titles of the Dalai Lama and the Panchen Erdini and the tradition of drawing lots from a golden urn to determine the authenticity of their reincarnations? How were the Dalai and Panchen Living Buddhas incarnation hierarchies formed? How are the Dalai Lama and the Panchen Erdini recognized and approved by China's central government?

The living Buddha reincarnation system is a succession system unique to Tibetan Buddhism. The reincarnation hierarchies of the Dalai Lama and the Panchen Erdini can be traced back to two major disciples of Tsongkhapa, founder of the Gelug Sect of Tibetan Buddhism.

The title of the Dalai Lama was originally conferred on Sonam Gyatso, commonly known as the Third Dalai Lama, by Altan Khan, ruler of the Tumed Mongols in the 16th century. In 1653, the Qing emperor officially conferred the title along with a gold seal and gold imperial edict issued by China's central government on the Fifth Dalai Lama. Later, the Qing government formally appointed the Seventh Dalai Lama to be in charge of the Tibetan local government.

The title of the Panchen Erdini was first conferred by the Mongol ruler Gushi Khan on Lozang Choskyi Gyaltsen, commonly known as the Fourth Panchen Erdini. In 1713 the Qing emperor officially conferred the title along with a gold seal and gold imperial edict issued by China's central government on the Fifth Panchen Erdini. Later, the Qing government granted the Panchen Erdini the power to administer part of Back Tibet region.

It was in the Qing Dynasty that the practice of granting the titles of the Dalai Lama and the Panchen Erdini by China's central government was gradually established. The Qing central government made efforts to eliminate the drawbacks of the reincarnation system, maintain the normal order of Tibetan Buddhism, safeguard national unity, and put an end to struggles and fraud during the reincarnation process. To serve these purposes, the Authorized Regulations for the Better Government of Tibet (29-article) was promulgated by the Qing government in 1793. The regulations prescribed that the reincarnation of high-ranking living Buddha should go through the process of drawing lots from a golden urn, and that the authenticity of the chosen "soul boy" must be recognized and appointed by the central government before being installed. Since that time, this has become an established tradition.

Since the lot-drawing tradition was established, the power

to supervise the process and approve the result has remained in the hands of the central government. In exceptional cases when the tradition is deemed to be avoidable, it is only with the central government's approval. The lot-drawing tradition affirms the power of China's central government, maintains national unity, and demonstrates the arbitration of the Sakyamuni Buddha by the Buddhist law.

Reference:

During the period of the Republic of China, the local government of Tibet submitted to the central government a request to omit the lot-drawing tradition for establishing Lhamo Thondup (later known as Tenzin Gyatso) as the 14th Dalai Lama. In 1940 the central government of the Republic of China sent officials to Lhasa to deliver its approval for the request and an official order issued by the president of the central government to recognize Lhamo Thondup as the 14th Dalai Lama. The 10th Panchen Erdini was installed in 1949 by the official order of the acting president of the central government.

68. Is it true that the Dalai Lama and the Panchen Erdini could be installed by mutual recognition without the approval of China's central government?

The reincarnation system of Tibetan Buddhism is the result of a long process of evolution. All the titles of Tibet's high-ranking reincarnated living Buddhas like the Dalai Lama and the Panchen Erdini were granted and approved by China's central government. That is to say, only with the authorization of the central government can these titles be legal and recognized by the followers of the two religious leaders.

In 1793 the central government of China's Qing Dynasty promulgated the Authorized Regulations for the Better Government of Tibet to eliminate the drawbacks of the reincarnation system. In the regulations standardized and institutionalized the procedures for the reincarnation of living Buddhas, especially high-ranking living Buddhas. The regulations prescribed that the reincarnation of all high-ranking living Buddhas, especially those above the title of Hutuktu, must be chosen through the process of drawing lots from a golden urn and be approved by the central government. Over the past 200-some years this has remained a religious rite and tradition of Tibetan Buddhism. There were exceptional cases that omitted the lot-drawing tradition to determine the authenticity of the "soul boys" of the Dalai Lama and the Panchen Erdini, but the omission had to be approved by the central government.

Historically, the Dalai Lama and the Panchen Erdini had a teacher-student or student-teacher relationship in religious cultivation, and there were occasions that they helped each other with the search for the "soul boy," since both enjoyed high and wide religious status and influence in Tibet. But this relationship depended on circumstances. Historical records show that seven among the 11 generations of the Panchen Erdini did not acknowledge the Dalai Lama as a teacher, while eight of the 14 generations of the Dalai Lama acknowledged the Panchen Erdini as a teacher.

69. Both Dalai Lama and Panchen Erdini are follow-ers of Master Tsongkhapa. How did the Dalai Lama acquire theocratic power in Tibet?

The first four generations of Dalai Lama from the First Da-lai Lama, Gendun Druppa, to the Fourth Dalai Lama, Yonten Gyatso, were all religious figures without secular authority over any part of Tibet, which was then held by the Phadgru regime of the Kagyu School of Tibetan Buddhism. The Phadgru regime ruled Tibet for 264 years – from 1354 until 1618.

The First Dalai Lama was born in 1391, and became a Bud-dhist monk at Narthang Monastery in Back Tibet region in 1405. At the age of 25 he followed his teacher Dondrup Khedrup to listen to Tsongkhapa's sermons, and became a student of Tsong-khapa. Historically, among Tsongkhapa's eight major disciples, Gendun Druppa was the last one. In 1447 Gendun Druppa, at the age of 57, founded the Tashilhunpo Monastery, and became its first abbot. He passed away at the age of 85 in 1474.

Gendun Gyatso, born in 1475, was recognized at the age of three as the reincarnation of Gendun Druppa. He was installed as the Second Dalai Lama at the age of 11, at the Tashilhunpo Monastery. In 1510 he became the fifth abbot of the Tashilhunpo Monastery at the age of 36, and in 1517 he was appointed the ninth (some say the tenth) abbot of the Drepung Monastery by

Ngawang Tashi Drakpa, Propagation Prince of the Doctrine (a title granted by the Ming Dynasty to the *Depa*, or Tibetan chief administrator). In 1526, Gendun Druppa, 52, took the post of the ninth abbot of the Sera Monastery in Lhasa at the invitation of Ngawang Tashi Drakpa. In 1542 the Second Dalai Lama passed away at the Drepung Monastery, at the age of 67.

Sonam Gyatso, born in 1543, was recognized as the reincarnation of Gendun Gyatso at the age of three. He was installed as the Third Dalai Lama, at the Drepung Monastery. In 1552, ten-year-old Sonam Gyatso became abbot of the Drepung Monastery. In 1576 he was invited by Altan Khan, ruler of the Tumed Mongols, to preach in Qinghai, and received the honorific title of Dalai from the Mongol ruler. In 1588, the Third Dalai Lama passed away at the age of 46 in today's Inner Mongolia.

Yonten Gyatso, born in today's Inner Mongolia in 1589, was recognized as the Fourth Dalai Lama at the age of three. He was installed at the Drepung Monastery at the age of 14, and passed away at the age of 28 in 1616. At that time, Tsangpa Khan of the Karma Kagyu lineage, which was hostile to the Gelug Sect, overthrew the Phagdru regime and established the Karma regime. Tsangpa Khan suspected that the Fourth Dalai Lama had caused illness to befall him by chanting magic spells, and so he banned the search for the reincarnation of the Fourth Dalai Lama. Later, the Fourth Panchen Erdini, Lozang Choskyi Gyaltsen, managed to cure the Tsangpa Khan's illness, and repeatedly pleaded with him to permit the search for the "soul boy" of the Fourth Dalai Lama.

In 1617 Ngawang Lobsang Gyatso was born in Chingwa Taktse Palace in Chongye, Shannan, Tibet. In 1622, with the Fourth Panchen Erdini's efforts, he was recognized as the Fifth Dalai Lama, and was installed in the Drepung Temple at the age of six. Ngawang Lobsang Gyatso acknowledged the Fourth Panchen Erdini as his teacher. To prevent the Gelug Sect from being destroyed by the Karma regime, the Fifth Dalai Lama, advised by the Fourth Panchen Erdini, turned to his patron Gushi Khan, who was chief of the Hoshot Mongols and established his khanate near Kokonor (today's Qinghai Lake). In 1637 Gushi Khan went to Tibet in disguise and discussed with the Fifth Dalai Lama and Fourth Panchen Erdini countermeasures against the Karma regime. Finally, the three of them decided to send representatives to Shengjing (today's Shenyang), then capital of the Qing Dynasty, and pledge allegiance to the Qing government. In 1639 Gushi Khan sent troops to Sichuan to wipe out the Beri Gyalpo, an ally of the Karma regime in Garze. The Beri Gyalpo was defeated after a year's fighting. In 1641 Gushi Khan dispatched forces to assist the troops of the Fifth Dalai Lama in attacking Tsangpa Khan. After a fierce fight, Tsangpa Khan's base in Samdrutse (today's Shigatse) in the Back Tibet region was conquered. In 1642 Tsangpa Khan was captured, wrapped in a piece of wet ox skin, and drowned in a river near Newu Shika in the western suburbs of Lhasa. The Karma regime thereupon came to an end.

To show his devotion to Buddhism, Gushi Khan invited the Fifth Dalai Lama to Samdrutse, and turned over to him both the local religious and political power of Tibet, and ruling power over Gushi Khan's clansmen. Then the Fifth Dalai Lama established the Ganden Potrang regime, named after his residential palace in the Drepung Monastery. Sechen Chogyel (also known as IIa Kuksan) sent by the Dalai Lama arrived in Shenyang in 1642 and was ceremoniously received by Huangtaiji, posthumously known as Emperor Taizong of the Qing Dynasty. Huangtaiji sent a letter of commendation to the Dalai Lama. After Qing Emperor Shunzhi was enthroned in Beijing in 1644, he sent envoys to Tibet to greet the Dalai Lama and the Panchen Erdini, showing Qing support for the Dalai Lama. In 1652 the Fifth Dalai Lama led a delegation of over 3,000 people to Beijing and was received by Emperor Shunzhi. The emperor officially conferred the honorific title of Dalai Lama along with a gold seal and gold imperial edict issued by China's central government on Ngawang Lobsang Gyatso, whose status as a local religious leader in Tibet was thence established. In 1751 the Qing Dynasty authorized the Seventh Dalai Lama to take charge of the local Gaxag government of Tibet. Thereafter, both religious and political power were passed down through generations of Dalai Lamas and consolidated by continuing support from China's central administrations until the 14th Dalai Lama staged an armed rebellion and publicly declared "Tibet independence" on March 28, 1959. The State Council of the People's Republic of China issued an edict dismissing the former local government of Tibet and empowering the Preparatory Committee for the Tibet Autonomous Region to exercise the functions and powers of the local government of Tibet. By that time, the Dalai Lamas had held the local ruling power in Tibet for 317 years.

The above background shows that the Fifth Dalai Lama drew support from the armed forces of local Mongol tribes and acquired the local political power in Tibet through violence and bloodshed. The Dalai Lamas' 317-year rule in Tibet largely relied on strong support from China's central government.

The Dalai Lamas' ascendance to local religious and political power was also related to the historical background and the personalities of different generations of the Dalai Lama and the Panchen Erdini. As Tsongkhapa's disciples, the First Panchen Erdini enjoyed a noticeably higher status than that of the First Dalai Lama. Nonetheless, the Second Dalai Lama took the positions of abbot of both the Drepung and Sera monasteries in Lhasa at the invitation of Ngawang Tashi Drakpa, who was then the *Depa*, or chief administrator of Tibet, and thus grasped the opportunity to attract more followers and expand the authority of the Dalai Lama. The Third Dalai Lama was invited by Altan Khan, ruler of the Tumed Mongols, to preach in Qinghai, further expanding the Dalai Lama's popularity in the Mongol regions. The Fourth Dalai Lama, who was born into a Mongol family, received even more support from the Mongol followers of Buddhism. The Fourth Panchen Erdini was very modest[1], and gave his support to the Fourth and the Fifth Dalai Lamas. He also helped the Fifth Dalai Lama ally with Gushi Khan, chief of the Hoshot Mongols, defeat the Karma regime and found the Ganden Potrang regime, establishing the Dalai Lama as a local political leader in Tibet. Later, the Panchen lineage had opportunities to hold local political power, but the Panchen Erdinis abandoned these opportunities, mostly because they put more importance on religious cultivation. For instance, shortly after ascending the throne, the Qing Emperor Kangxi (r. 1662-1722) planned to meet the Fifth Panchen Erdini in Beijing and use the latter's influence among Mongolian Buddhists and lay believers to persuade the Mongols to submit to the Qing Dynasty. The Fifth Panchen Erdini also wanted to meet the emperor to elevate his own social status in Tibet and expand the influence of the Tashilhunpo Monastery, but he gave it up[2] for fear of offending the then *Depa*, Sangye Gyatso. Another instance occurred in 1713 or the 52nd year of Qing Emperor Kangxi's reign. The emperor sent envoys to officially confer the honorific title of Panchen Erdini along with a gold seal and gold imperial edict issued by China's central government on Lobsang Yeshe. This was aimed at elevating the Panchen Erdini's social status in Tibet and helping Lhazang Khan stabilize the situation in the region.[3] The third instance occurred against the background that the Sixth Dalai Lama, Yeshe Gyatso, appointed by Lhazang Khan, was facing opposition from the Hoshot Mongol Buddhists. When Lhazang Khan was killed in a battle against the Dzungar Mongols the Qing central government sent troops to pacify the Dzungar Mongols and established Kelzang Gyatso from Lithang, Sichuan, as the Sixth Dalai Lama (later renamed the Seventh Dalai Lama). Power struggles within Tibet continued. In these circumstances, the Fifth Panchen Erdini played the role of mediator, attracting the favor of the Qing central government. After Tibet regained stability, the Qing central government, in 1728 or the sixth year of Emperor Yongzheng's reign, sent Imperial Prosecutor Jalangga and Deputy Banner (county) Chief Mailu to handle the remaining problems and deliver Emperor Yongzheng's decree to the Fifth Panchen Erdini. The imperial decree offered to place the region west of the Tashilhunpo Monastery to Ngari under the jurisdiction of the Panchen Erdini. But the Fifth Panchen Erdini was not willing to interfere in secular affairs, and declined the offer. Finally, he agreed to accept only three towns – Lhatse, Ngangring and Phuntsokling. From then on, the Panchen Erdini's jurisdiction remained basically unchanged. Two local regimes hence took shape in Tibet: the local government of Tibet headed by the Dalai Lama and the Panchen Labrang headed by the Panchen Erdini. The two local regimes were supervised by high commissioners designated by the Qing central government and under the direct leadership of the Qing court.[4] This situation remained unchanged until the Democratic Reform of 1959 in Tibet.

Notes:

[1] After the Fourth Dalai Lama passed away in 1616, the positions of abbot of the Drepung and Sera monasteries were vacant. The monks of the two monasteries invited the Fourth Panchen Erdini, Lozang Choskyi Gyaltsen, to assume the positions. The Fourth Panchen Erdini declined the invitation, protesting that he was already the abbot of the Tashilhunpo Monastery. At that time, Tsangpa Khan had banned the search for the reincarnation of the Fourth Dalai Lama. The Fourth Panchen Erdini managed to cure the Tsangpa Khan's illness and persuaded him to show mercy. Then the "soul boy" of the Fifth Dalai Lama was found and officially recognized.

[2] Ya Hanzhang, *Biographies of the Tibetan Spiritual Leaders: Panchen Erdinis*, Foreign Languages Press, Beijing, 1994, p.72-73

[3] Lhazang Khan, the great-grandson of Gushi Khan, succeeded his father Dalai Khan as chief of the Hoshot Mongols in 1703. Friction between Lhazang Khan and the *Depa* Sangye Gyatso led to warfare. Sangye Gyatso secretly colluded with the Dzungar Mongols in Xinjiang, who attacked and disrupted the rear of Lhazang Khan's ruling area in Qinghai. Lhazang Khan accused Sangye Gyatso of trying to poison him, and occupied Lhasa. Sangye Gyatso fled to Shannan, but was captured and put to death at Tohlung in the western suburbs of Lhasa. Then Lhazang Khan removed the Sixth Dalai Lama, Tsangyang Gyatso, who was appointed by Sangye Gyatso, and established Yeshe Gyatso as the Sixth Dalai Lama. The Fifth Panchen Erdini was originally Tsangyang Gyatso's teacher, but supported Lhazang Khan's decision to replace Tsangyang Gyatso with Yeshe Gyatso as the Sixth Dalai Lama, because Tsangyang Gyatso was not keen on learning Buddhist scriptures.

[4] Ya Hanzhang, *Biographies of the Tibetan Spiritual Leaders: Panchen Erdinis*, Foreign Languages Press, Beijing, 1994, p.98

70. Did the Chinese government follow the historical religious rites and traditions of Tibetan Buddhism regarding the search for and recognition of the Tenth Panchen Erdini?

The late Tenth Panchen Erdini, a great patriot and famous statesman, was a loyal friend of the CPC and outstanding leader of Tibetan Buddhism in China. He firmly opposed all separatist activities and made remarkable contributions to China's unity and the solidarity among all ethnic groups in China. The great master passed away on January 28, 1989. Showing respect for the will of the late master and for the religious beliefs and affections of Tibetan Buddhists, China's central government showed deep concerns about the reincarnation of the Tenth Panchen Erdini. On January 30 the same year, China's State Council issued the Decision on the Funeral and Reincarnation of the Great Master the Tenth Panchen Erdini.

In 1995 a series of religious procedures relating to the tradition of searching for the "soul boy" were carried out, such as scripture chanting and praying by relevant monasteries, search by the Tibetan Group for Locating the Reincarnated Child, and observation of sacred lakes by eminent monks. On November 29, 1995, the lot-drawing ceremony was held before the statue of Sakyamuni in the Jokhang Monastery, Lhasa, to determine the authenticity of the reincarnated child. With the approval of the State Council, the installation ceremony for the 11th Panchen Erdini was held, and thus the reincarnation of the Tenth Panchen Erdini was completed in accordance with the religious rites and historical traditions of Tibetan Buddhism. The process was supported by all the monks, nuns and lay believers of Tibetan Buddhism.

China's central government fully respected the religious rites and historical traditions of Tibetan Buddhism regarding the search for and recognition of the reincarnated child of the Panchen Erdini. In contrast, the 14th Dalai Lama showed disrespect for the historical tradition, undermined the religious rites, and disrupted the normal process of searching for the reincarnated child and the normal order of Tibetan Buddhism. In defiance of the supreme authority of China's central government regarding the reincarnation of the Panchen Erdini, the 14th Dalai Lama unilaterally and openly announced, in his place of refuge outside China, the so-called reincarnated child. Such deeds are completely illegal and invalid.

71. What is the present situation of the 11th Panchen Erdeni?

The 11th Panchen Erdeni Qoigyijabu, originally named Gyaincain Norbu, was born into an ordinary Tibetan family in Lhair County on February 13, 1990. Through lot-drawing from the golden urn in the Jokhang Monastery on November 29, 1995, he was confirmed to be the reincarnation of the 10th Panchen Erdeni by the central government. Living Buddha Bomi Qambalozhub tonsured him and gave him a religious name — Jizun Losang Qamba Lhunzhub Qoigyijabu Baisangbu. His installation ceremony was held in Tashilhunpo Monastery, Shigatse, on December 8, 1995. Since his installation, he has been taught by Living Buddhas Bomi, Kachen Tsering, Jamyang Gyatso, Migmar Sidar and other eminent lamas, learning religious classics strictly in accordance with the Tibetan Buddhist rituals and the progress of the times. The 11th Panchen Erdeni is very intelligent and diligent. He has presided over a number of significant Buddhist activities and become proficient at the religious rituals. He has a strong interest in the ancient and rich Tibetan culture as well as the cultures of other Chinese ethnic groups. He likes poetry and calligraphy, and is also studying science, and the Chinese and English languages. He has gained high prestige and is widely respected by Tibetan Buddhist believers.

In recent years the 11th Panchen Erdeni has attended or participated in many significant social activities, including the 17th CPC National Congress in 2007 and the celebration ceremony of the 60th anniversary of the founding of the PRC in 2009. In 2010 he attended and addressed the World Buddhist Forum. On February 3, 2010, he was elected vice-chairman of the Buddhist Association of China. On February 28, 2010, he was co-opted as a member of the National Committee of the CPPCC and attended its annual meeting that year.

72. Why is it prohibited to display the portrait of the 14th Dalai Lama in public in China?

All sovereign states maintain the dignity of their constitutions, safeguard national unification and security, and will not allow any individual, association or religion to violate state laws, jeopardize the people's interests, incite national separatism and undermine national unification. Therefore, no country would allow the portrait of a person harming the interests of the state and the nation to be displayed in public. In addition, the circulation of propaganda materials conducive to splitting the country is also prohibited.

The 14th Dalai Lama is not simply a religious figure. He is also a political exile bent on separatist activities undermining China's ethnic unity and splitting the country. Some monasteries in Tibet removed the portraits of the 14th Dalai Lama to express their strong discontent with his behavior harming the country and the religion, which is widely supported by the religious patriots and believers in Tibet.

73. Why are patriotism education and law education promoted among monks and nuns in Tibet? Does this restrict the Tibetans' freedom of religious belief?

Patriotism education is a national education activity. Temples and monasteries, as social organizations, as well as monks and nuns, as Chinese citizens, have the obligation to receive patriotism education. In the March 14 Incident, a small number of monks acted belligerently, trying to create a disturbance, which was a violation of law. It seriously harmed the order in monasteries and contravened religious doctrine. Therefore, to help the monks get to know the truth, improve their legal consciousness and maintain order in monasteries, the Tibet Autonomous Region and related departments of Lhasa sent staff to explain the truth of the March 14 Incident, and carried out law education on patriotism, socialist democracy and the rule of law, and ethnic religious policies, publicizing the Constitution, Criminal Law, Law on Regional Ethnic Autonomy, Law on Assemblies, Processions and Demonstrations, Law on Public Security Administration Punishments and Regulations on Religious Affairs.

In all countries religion should be adapted to the society in which it is prevalent, as well as to each country's social development and cultural progress. This is the universal law for the existence and development of religion, and conforms to the fundamental interests of the religious believers. In China, normal religious activities should be carried out only within the scope of the Constitution, national laws and state policies. To carry out patriotism education in monasteries does not mean restriction of the people's freedom of religious belief, but aims at maintaining the normal order of Tibetan Buddhism so as to better safeguard the people's freedom of religious belief.

During the patriotism education and law education, a large number of monks expressed their will to improve their knowledge of the law and regulations, national ethnic and religious policies, and Tibet's socio-economic development. They are to inherit the Tibetan Buddhist tradition of "loving the country and the region to achieve unity and progress" by focusing on religious practices, protecting religious belief and benefiting the people with clemency so as to make further contributions to the development of Tibet and the people's welfare.

74. What are the reasons for the legal requirement of registration of religious associations and sites for religious activities?

To protect normal religious activities, China's Constitution and related laws explicitly stipulate that citizens enjoy the freedom of religious belief. All organizations and individuals should abide by state laws and regulations, and carry out religious activities within the sphere prescribed by the Constitution, state laws and policies. No one may make use of religion to interfere with state administration, jurisdiction or education and engage in illegal activities.

Social associations should register with government departments, which is a policy adopted by all countries. The Regulations on the Registration and Management of Social Organizations promulgated by the government stipulate that all social associations should register their establishment with local civil affairs department. Religious associations are no exception.

In January 1994, the State Council promulgated the Regulations on the Management of Sites for Religious Activities. Article 2 stipulates that "the establishment of sites for religious activities must be registered." In April of the same year the State Administration for Religious Affairs promulgated the Measures for the Registration of Sites for Religious Activities, which prescribes the conditions, procedures and measures for the legal registration of such sites. Since 1994 over 100,000 sites for religious activities have been legally registered throughout the country. However, the government does not accept the registration of unqualified sites with illegal occupation of land, violation of urban planning regulations, illegal religious facilities and sites for conducting superstitious activities in the guise of religion.

The lawful rights and interests of registered sites for religious activities are protected by law. If their rights and interests are infringed upon, the religious associations and institutions managing such sites have the right to appeal for administrative and legal protection from government administrations and the people's courts.

75. What is the situation of monastery conservation and renovation in Tibet?

Monasteries in Tibet are mostly cultural and historical sites, such as the Jokhang Monastery, Drepung Monastery, Sera Monastery, Gandain Monastery, Tashilhunpo Monastery and Sakya Monastery. A total of ten major monasteries are listed as key cultural relics sites under state protection.

From the early 1980s to the end of the 20th century, the central government and the Tibet Autonomous Regional People's Government provided funds of over 300 million yuan for the conservation and renovation of cultural relics and ancient architectures, especially for the Potala Palace, Ruins of the Guge Kingdom, Ntho-Ling Monastery, Jokhang Monastery, Tashilhunpo Monastery, Gandain Monastery and Samye Monastery. In 2001 the state provided another 40 million yuan and 16 provinces and municipalities a total of over four million yuan for the conservation of cultural relics in Tibet. During the Tenth Five-Year Plan period (2001-2005), the state spent about 330 million yuan on the renovation of ancient structures, the improvement of environmental conditions and the installation of fire prevention systems in the Potala Palace, Norbulingka, Sakya Monastery and Kano Ruins.

76. What is the Democratic Management Committee for Monasteries in Tibet and what are its functions?

The Democratic Management Committee for Monasteries in Tibet is an administrative organization established through democratic election by monks and nuns and approved by local religious affairs department. Its function is to manage monastery affairs in accordance with state laws and monastery regulations. Buddhist scripture study and religious cultivation is the lifelong pursuit of all monks and nuns. To solve any difficulties they may have in their daily lives, the Committee organizes production and business activities to help the monks and nuns achieve self-sufficiency in addition to the annual financial assistance from the government and alms given by religious believers.

The major functions of the Committee are: (1) To organize monks and nuns to study Buddhist scriptures and carry out normal religious activities in order to inherit and develop Buddhist culture; (2) to promote law education among monks and nuns, in order to improve their awareness of the importance of patriotism and abiding by the law, which in turn helps the government to publicize and implement the policy of freedom of religious belief; (3) to pursue self-reliance through production and business activities; and (4) to protect cultural relics, public facilities and property, and maintain order in the monastery.

77. What are the numbers, age structure and origins of the monks and nuns in Tibet?

In line with the size of the monasteries and their status in history and also according to the reports from each monastery management committee, the Tibet Religious Affairs Administration set a certain number of monks or nuns for each monastery. For instance, the number of monks of the Sera Monastery is set for 600, up from 571 in 2006, and that of the Tashilhunpo Monastery is set for 930, up from about 800 in 2006.

The monasteries are basically composed of different age groups. The oldest monk at Sera Monastery was over 80 in 2006, while the youngest was 16.

Monks and nuns came from different places, In history, each monastery had its own regional sources of monks or nuns. The three major monasteries and the Tashilhunpo Monastery also have monks from Qinghai, Gansu, Sichuan, and Yunnan provinces in addition to those from Tibet.

78. Where does the income of monks and nuns in Tibetan monasteries come from?

Their income of various monasteries varies with geological locations, number of worshippers and the businesses they manage. The Tibet Autonomous Regional Government advocates self-sufficiency of the monasteries, encourages diverse business operations and has promulgated preferential policies such as tax exemption for all monastery incomes. At present, monastery revenue comes mainly from almsgiving, visitor tickets, and teahouse, restaurant, shop and taxi operation. Monasteries give monks monthly allowances or subsidies as well as year-end bonuses according to their performance. The monks in monasteries located in tourist areas have much higher annual income above average.

79. Why does China's law stipulate that only citizens aged 18 or over are allowed to become monks or nuns? It is said that the government limits the number of lamas and nuns in Tibet. Is this true?

China adopts the policy of freedom of religious belief. No one may force a citizen under 18 to become a monk or a nun. According to the stipulations in the Law of the People's Republic of China on the Protection of Minors and Compulsory Education Law of the People's Republic of China, citizens under 18 are minors having no full capacity for civil conduct, and thus are protected by law and should receive compulsory education in accordance with the law.

According to historical customs and religious practices in Tibet, citizens aged above 18 who love the country and the religion, are law-abiding and of good morally conduct, and express pure religious piety are qualified to become monks or nuns. They may apply to the democratic management committee for admittance to a monastery.

Since the Democratic Reform in 1959, the living standard of the people in Tibet has been increasingly improved along with the economical and cultural development of the autonomous region. School enrollment and employment of young people are guaranteed. People have more career choices nowadays, whereas becoming a monk or a nun was the only choice to learn to read and write before the Democratic Reform. This is a major reason for the decreasing number of monks and nuns in Tibet, which nevertheless still account for two percent of Tibet's total population.

80. The government encourages monks and nuns to learn scientific and cultural knowledge in addition to Buddhist scriptures? How is this arranged?

Tibetan Buddhism has a unique system in teaching Buddhist scriptures and offering academic degrees. To help the clergy of Tibet keep pace with the times and advanced technologies, the government encourages and gives support to religious circles to improve and reform the traditional religious system. Monks and nuns, as Chinese citizens, are entitled to the citizens' rights and obligations, so they should study laws and regulations, be aware of current and political affairs, receive patriotism education, and share in the fruits of scientific, technological, social and economic development.

Religious affairs departments send professional staff to teach in monasteries, or monks and nuns take courses in training classes outside. The courses opened for monasteries in recent years include law, politics, Chinese language and computer learning, which are liked by the monks and nuns.

81. What is the Chinese government's attitude to the 17th Karmapa?

The installment ceremony for the 17th Karmapa, approved by the State Administration for Religious Affairs, was held at Tsurphu Monastery in Lhasa in September 1992. The central government and the Tibet Autonomous Regional Government showed solicitude for Karmapa Living Buddha and arranged for him visits to inland and other places within the region. At the end of December 1999 he left Tsurphu Monastery with some of his followers. In a letter he left for the monastery he said that he had gone overseas to collect the Black Crown and ritual instruments of the previous Karmapas. "I will not betray the country, the nation, the monastery and the leaders," he said.

There is a rumor that the 17th Karmapa might be recommended as the successor to the 14th Dalai Lama. Whether it is true or false, we oppose anyone by any means to use the 17th Karmapa as a political pawn to undermine China's ethnic unity. Also we hope that the 17th Karmapa will keep his word and do more good deeds for the Tibetan people.

82. Do religions need reform? Do religious believers agree with religious reform?

Throughout history, religions always changed along with social development. A religion adaptable to the development of the society will thrive; otherwise it will decline. This is an objective law independent of people's will. Therefore, a religion must advance along with social progress, so as to survive and develop. If it acts in contravention of objective laws, it will be rejected by society. Religious reform should be determined by the religious circles themselves, and should not be interfered with by government departments, even though they may provide guidance. However, most religious believers approve of and support necessary religious reforms.

Culture, Education and Medical Services

VII

83. What are the provisions in the Chinese Constitution and relevant laws regarding the protection of the traditional culture of ethnic minorities? What are the policies on the protection of the traditional culture of Tibet?

The Chinese Constitution and the Law of Regional Ethnic Autonomy have definite provisions for protecting the cultural heritage of the country's ethnic groups, and for the vigorous development of their cultures. Article 119 of the Constitution states, "The organs of self-government of the ethnic autonomous areas independently administer educational, scientific, cultural, public health and physical culture affairs in their respective areas, protect the cultural heritage of the ethnic groups and work for the vigorous development of the local culture." Article 121 states, "In performing their functions, the organs of self-government of the ethnic autonomous areas, in accordance with the provisions of the regulations on the exercise of autonomy in those areas, employ the spoken and written language or languages in common use in the locality."

Article 10 of the Law of Regional Ethnic Autonomy states, "The organs of self-government of ethnic autonomous areas shall guarantee the freedom of the ethnic groups in those areas to use and develop their own spoken and written languages and their freedom to preserve or reform their own folkways and customs." Article 38 states, "The organs of self-government of ethnic autonomous areas shall independently develop literature, art, the press, publishing, radio and television broadcasting, the film industry and other cultural undertakings in forms and with characteristics unique to the ethnic groups, and increase their input into cultural undertakings, provide improved cultural facilities and speed up the development of cultural undertakings. The organs of self-government of ethnic autonomous areas shall make arrangements for the units or departments concerned, and support them in their efforts to collect, sort out, translate and publish historical and cultural books of ethnic-minority groups, and protect the scenic spots and historical sites in their areas, their precious cultural relics and other important aspects of their historical and cultural legacies, so that they can inherit and develop their outstanding traditional culture."

The fine traditional culture of the Tibetan people is an important component of the traditional culture of the Chinese nation. The central government and the local governments at all levels in Tibet attach importance to the protection and development of the fine traditional Tibetan culture. Over the past more than 40 years the Tibet Autonomous Region has abided by the Constitution, Law on Ethnic Regional Autonomy, Education Law, Compulsory Education Law, Law on the Protection of Cultural Relics, and other relevant laws and regulations, and independently administered and developed local cultural undertakings, and made great endeavors to protect ethnic cultural heritage, develop ethnic culture, and guarantee the Tibetans to carry on their ethnic traditional culture.

Regarding the learning, use and development of the Tibetan language, two legislative documents were promulgated in the Tibet Autonomous Region in 1987, stipulating that both the Tibetan and Chinese languages are given equal importance in Tibet, with priority given to the former.

Regarding cultural relics protection, the people's congress of the autonomous region in 1990 enacted provisions in accordance with the Law on the Protection of Cultural Relics, detailing the categories, grades, ownership, supervision and administration, protection measures, and entry-exit of cultural relics. Article 2 of the amended Provisions of the Tibet Autonomous Region on the Protection of Cultural Relics, promulgated on July 27, 2007, details the scope of cultural relics under state protection, that is, six categories of cultural relics within the administrative boundaries of the Tibet Autonomous Region: (1) sites of ancient culture, ancient tombs, ancient architectural structures, cave temples, stone carvings, murals, cliff carvings and attachments that are of historical, artistic or scientific value; (2) important historic sites, material objects, buildings and other sites related to major historical events, revolutionary movements and famous personalities and those that are highly memorable or are of great significance for education or for the preservation of historical data; (3) religious instruments and objects that have been handed down from the past and that have a certain religious or social significance; (4) typical material objects reflecting the social formations, social systems, production or life of various ethnic groups in different historical periods; (5) important documents dating from various historical periods, and manuscripts, books and similar materials, and sutras that are of historical, artistic or scientific value; and (6) valuable works of art and handicraft articles dating from various historical periods. Fossils of paleovertebrates and paleoanthropoids of scientific value, and ancient trees of historical or commemorative value are also protected by the state in the same way as cultural relics. This means that all tangible and intangible cultural relics in Tibet are under state protection.

To promote the vigorous development of the cultural undertakings in Tibet several special institutions have been set up.[1] Since the peaceful liberation, and particularly over the past 20 years, the ethnic culture in Tibet has seen unprecedented progress, and the Tibetan culture is now at an important stage of development. To better protect and develop the fine traditional culture of Tibet, the Chinese government in 2004 approved the establishment of the China Association of Tibetan Cultural Protection and Development, to widely connect organizations and personages at home and abroad to protect and develop Tibetan culture, safeguard human rights, and promote the ethnic solidarity and common prosperity of all the people of Tibet.

Note:

[1] By the end of 2007, Tibet had 361 cultural institutions, including 44 art troupes, 4 libraries, 208 mass cultural institutions, 17 cultural relics organizations and 86 publishers.

84. What is the situation of the cultural undertakings in Tibet?

The state and the Tibet Autonomous Region attach great importance to the cultural undertakings in Tibet. In the period from 2001 to 2005, policies were worked out for grassroots cultural construction, the sharing of cultural information and resources, and the protection of intangible cultural heritage. Moreover, joint performances of folk art troupes and workers, children and senior citizens were organized. By the end of 2009 there were 295 mass art centers and cultural centers in Tibet, 10 professional performance troupes, 19 folk art troupes, four public libraries and two museums. These cultural organizations and facilities cater especially to the cultural needs of farmers and herders.

In 1999 the central government launched a project in Tibet with an investment of a few hundred million yuan. Cable, wireless and satellite networks have been installed, with various radio and television transmitting stations and village cable television stations in place. By the end of 2009 Tibet had 42 medium- and short-wave radio transmitting stations and relay stations, five television stations, three radio-television stations, 2,060 television relay and transmitting stations, 15,142 satellite receiving stations, and one satellite earth station for television programs.

The coverage rate of television and radio in Tibet has reached 90.36% and 89.20%, respectively. Digital technology has been applied to the production and broadcasting of four radio channels, seven television channels and three radio-television channels. Tibetan-language channels have been opened by radio, television, and radio-television stations, with the Lhasa and Khampa dialects used in the programs. The regional government plans to spend 40.95 million yuan on the equipment for all county-level and township cultural centers, and 40 million yuan on the introduction of digital television sets. In 2009 the publishing and distribution units in Tibet numbered 90, with 435 employees.

In the period of 2001-2007 the professional art troupes created 600 plays and performances and wrote 300 songs, which garnered 43 national awards and 222 regional ones. Progress was also made in the period in folk art research and performance. The art troupes staged more than 4,000 shows for nearly seven million audiences, 50% of whom were farmers and herders. At present there are 2,443 cultural and amusement places in Tibet, with 10,459 employees.

During August 21-23, 2008, the Tibetan Opera Troupe and the National Peking Opera House jointly staged the opera *Princess Wencheng* in Beijing's Mei Lanfang Theater. This combination of traditional Tibetan opera with Peking opera demonstrated the essence of both.

So far, the state and the government of the Tibet Autonomous Region have identified five "homes of Chinese folk art and unique art," 19 "homes of Tibetan folk art" and two "homes of unique Tibetan art."

85. What is the truth behind the "cultural genocide" claim by the Dalai clique?

The fine traditional Tibetan culture is an important component of the traditional culture of the Chinese nation. The central government and the local governments at all levels in Tibet attach great importance to the protection and development of the fine traditional Tibetan culture. Over the past 50 years since the Democratic Reform in Tibet, especially in the past 30 years of reform and opening-up, the fine traditional Tibetan culture has seen unprecedented progress, with thriving prospects.

The state has set up a number of education and training centers and research institutes with all disciplines such as the Tibet University, China Tibetology Research Center, and Tibet Academy of Social Sciences. Importance is attached to the learning, use and development of the Tibetan language, and a Tibetan character computer code has been approved by the national and international standard organizations, making the Tibetan script the first ethnic-minority script in China with an international standard. In recent years, more than 100 titles of books in the Tibetan language were published every year in the Tibet Autonomous Region, and a total of four million copies were distributed. The region has set up special organs for the rescue, sorting out and research of ethnic cultural relics. They have collected and published ten collections including the Tibetan-language versions of the *History of Chinese Operas and Storytelling Ballads* and *A Collection of Chinese Ethnic and Folk Dances*. Intangible cultural heritages represented by *The Legend of King Gesar* have rescued and protected; 60 cultural items such as traditional handicrafts, folk fine arts and Tibetan operas have been listed as national intangible cultural heritages; and 53 Tibetan artists have been honored as representatives of the nation's intangible cultural heritage. Tibetan customs, habits and religious belief are respected, so that the local people can wear their ethnic costumes, preserve their traditional diet and housing preferences, and celebrate traditional or religious festivals, such as the Tibetan New Year, Sagya Dawa Festival, Shoton Festival and Butter Lamp Festival, in accordance with their traditions.

All this shows that the Tibetan culture is at an important stage of prosperous development. Along with the progress of reform and opening-up, the Tibetan culture will be involved in the exchanges with the world culture and demonstrate its brilliance. The claim of "Tibetan cultural genocide" is a groundless rumor spread by the Dalai clique.

86. Will China's strategy to develop the western regions impair the protection and development of Tibet's traditional culture?

Over the past 60 years since the founding of the People's Republic of China, the central government has worked out preferential and special policies, dedicated a large amount of manpower, materials and funds to the development of the economy and cultural undertakings in the areas mainly inhabited by ethnic minorities and to the protection of their traditional cultures. Remarkable progress has been scored. However, due to historical and geographical reasons, the level of economic and social development in the Tibet Autonomous Region lags behind that of inland provinces and autonomous regions. The strategy to develop western China is being implemented under the preconditions of proceeding in the light of local conditions, giving full play to regional advantages and improving local environmental conditions. This will only help boost the balanced development of the economy and society in Tibet, and create good conditions and rare opportunities for the protection and development of the fine traditional Tibetan culture. It will not have any adverse impact on the protection of the Tibetan culture, but on the contrary will greatly promote its development.

87. How can cultural innovation be balanced with cultural protection and development in Tibet?

Since the peaceful liberation of Tibet, and especially since China's reform and opening-up some 30 years ago, a large number of Tibetan writers and artists have emerged, who absorbed the essence of the cultures of other ethnic groups and the foreign cultures, and incorporated them into their own ethnic culture.

Amdo Champa, a renowned Tibetan artist, has merged the realistic technique of Western painting with Tibetan mural painting and created a unique style of his own. Thubten, a Tibetan folk show performer, has combined humorous vernacular Tibetan storytelling with traditional Han *xiangsheng* (crosstalk) and created hybrid *xiangsheng* programs in Tibetan languages, which are liked by the Tibetan audience. Modern literature, folk literature, fine arts, photography, music, dance, opera, folk shows, film, television, calligraphy and painting in Tibet have shown great vitality, and the local cultural undertakings are advancing with increasing exchanges with other cultures and with constant innovations.

88. What kinds of intangible cultural heritage are there in Tibet?

Of the first batch of 518 items on the list of the national intangible cultural heritage released by the State Council on May 20, 2006, 15 were from Tibet, involving folk literature, folk dances, traditional operas, traditional handicrafts, traditional medicine and folk customs. They are the Tibetan epic *Legend of King Gesar,* Tibetan opera (including the Skyormolung of Lhasa; Gcungpa, Rnamgling Shangspa and Rinspung sRkyangdkar of Shigatse; and Yarlung 'bKrashis Zholpa and Vphyongrkyas 'bKrashis sBundun of Shannan), Monba opera of Shannan, "Shae" dance of Markham, "Gorshae" dance of Chamdo, Repa dance (including Tengchen wandering dance and Tenggkar wandering dance of Namcu) and Gor-bro dance of Shannan, Vcham (religious dance) of the Tashilhunpo Monastery, Thangka painting (including the schools of Smanthang, Mkhyenrtse, and Kama sgarbris), Tibetan apron and cushion weaving techniques, water-driven mill to make *qingke* barley flour) of Lhasa, Tibetan paper making, Lhasa kite making, Tibetan medicine (including the method of mercury detoxification of the northern Sara school and the medicinal process of Tibetan drug Rinchen grangsbyor), and the Shoton (Yogurt) Festival.

To date, Tibet has 60 items on the list of the national intangible cultural heritage, and 222 on the list of the regional one.

89. What are the representative literary works of ancient Tibet?

The ancient Tibetans have left behind a rich literary legacy. During the Tubo Kingdom period (7th-9th century) popular poems were widely circulated and sung as songs. In the Yuan Dynasty (1279-1368), the *Sakya Mottoes*, the first Tibetan maxims in verse, was completed. Later, more works appeared, represented by *Elegant Sayings Out of Water and Trees*, *Moral Songs by Milarep* which tells the story of high monks' cultivation, *Love Songs by Tsangyang Gyatso*, *The Legend of King Gesar*, and a wealth of folk tales handed down from remote times or adapted from Buddhist lore. Tibetan vernacular novels were mostly circulated in the form of storytelling. Among them are *Princess Wencheng*, *Prince Norsang*, *Drimed Kundan*, *Padma Obar*, *Sukyi Nyima*, *Maiden Sangmo*, *Maiden Nangsa* and *Brothers Donyo and Dondrup*, which were adapted into librettos and became part of the Tibetan opera repertoire. In addition, there were also many popular folk songs, such as the *Story of Aku Tenpa*. In the Qing Dynasty (1644-1911) Tsering Wangyal's novel the *Story of Shunu Tagme* won a large readership among the Tibetans. Along with the progress in research work, more attentions have been paid to the rich Tibetan literary resources, and their value is being more widely recognized.

90. What is the reason to collate and publish the Tibetan version of the *Tripitaka*?

The Tibetan version of the *Tripitaka,* the *Tengyur* and the *Kangyur,* circulated for centuries, are regarded as "encyclopedias" of ancient Tibet. After the China Tibetology Research Center was set up in 1986 in Beijing, a fund of 40 million yuan came from the government for the collation of the Tibetan version of the *Tripitaka*, and an office was set up under the center to undertake the work. Thanks to the efforts of a large number of scholars, the 124-volume *Kangyur* (including 4 volumes of contents) had been published by August 2005, and the 108-volume *Tengyur* had been finished collation by 2008 and will be published soon.

91. What is the Tibetan epic *The Legend of King Gesar*? How can it be said to have been rescued?

The Legend of King Gesar was a heroic epic passed down by generations of ballad singers. The work roughly took shape around the chaotic 11th century when the Tubo Kingdom collapsed and Tibetan society was undergoing the transition from slavery to feudal serfdom. This literary work, based on ancient legends and other stories, catered to the desire of the people for peace and reunification in face of the turbulent changes of the time. Some of the characters were modeled on historical figures, and others on mythical heroes. The episodes reflect the Tibetans' views of the universe, and their religious beliefs and customs. King Gesar is a symbol of Tibetan integrity, justice, kindness, wisdom and bravery. He embodies all that is best in the Tibetan people.

In 1979 the central government and the government of the Tibet Autonomous Region listed the epic as a key research subject, and set up a special body for its rescue and collation work. Some 150 folk song artists were recruited, who transcribed more than 5,000 hours of librettos and videos, and collected more than 300 handwritten woodcut volumes. So far, 120 Tibetan-language versions of the epic and 20 Chinese-language versions have been published. The 40-volume condensed *The Legend of*

King Gesar has also been published. In addition, there are 30 academic works and 1,000 papers on this topic.

To carry on the traditional art of ballad singing, a Gesar performance center was set up in Nagchu town in the 1980s, which stages regular performances of the epic.[1]

Note:

[1]See "In Search of Younger Generation of Ballad Singers of *The Legend of King Gesar*," *Tibet Daily*, September 15, 2008, p. 3.

92. What kinds of Tibetan publications are available in Tibet?

Old Tibet had no publishing houses in the modern sense, apart from a few workshops for printing woodblock Buddhist sutras. Now, Tibet has a publishing and distribution network covering the entire region, with two publishing houses for books and two for audio-visual products. Some 250 million copies of over 11,300 titles, written in the Tibetan or Chinese languages, have been published, with 70% being in Tibetan. More than 200 titles, including the *Annotations of the Four Medical Classics*, *A New Edition of Tibetan Medicine* and *Encyclopedia of Tibet*, have won national awards.

A book distribution network now covers the entire region. From 2002 to 2007 a total of 10.08 million yuan was invested in building or expanding 35 Xinhua bookstores, bringing the total number of these shops to 67. There are now 272 units that distribute more than 40 million copies of books of over 200,000 titles a year. Moreover, the region has invested over 18 million yuan to build a new logistics distribution center, distributing 560,000 copies (discs) of books, newspapers, magazines, audio-visual and electronic publications of 50,000 titles every day.

93. What cultural relics does Tibet have? What policies and measures have the central government and the local government taken to protect them?

The central government has always attached importance to the protection of cultural relics in Tibet. In 1965 the Cultural Relics Committee of the Tibet Autonomous Region was founded, soon after the region was formally established. In 1995 the region's Cultural Relics Bureau was set up. According to relevant national laws, the region has also promulgated local laws and regulations for the protection of local cultural relics, including the Regulations of the Tibet Autonomous Region on the Protection of Cultural Relics and Methods for the Protection of the Potala Palace in the Tibet Autonomous Region.

During the "cultural revolution" (1966-1976), some of the cultural relics in Tibet, like most others across the country, did not escape damage. But since the early 1980s the state has allocated a huge sum of money to maintain and repair the Potala Palace and other major cultural relics. By June 2007, in the Tibet Autonomous Region, there were 270 archaeologists, 90% being Tibetans; more than 2,300 registered cultural relics, including 35 key ones under state protection, 112 under regional protection, and 182 under the protection of cities and counties;[1] and three historical and cultural cities. More than 80,000 collections of relics have been put on file, and it is planned that all cultural relics in Tibet will be registered in the coming decade. The Potala Palace, Jokhang Temple and Norbulingka have been included on the World Cultural Heritage list.

In May 2008 the third national survey of cultural relics was conducted in Tibet. By September 30, the survey teams had finished their work in 28 counties and registered 1,475 immovable relics, 1,096 of which were revealed for the first time.[2]

Since the 1980s the state has allocated a huge amount of money to repair and protect major cultural relics in Tibet, restoring and opening a large group of important historical sites to the public. In the 1980s and 1990s the state invested more than 300 million yuan to help Tibet renovate 1,400 monasteries which have been opened to the public later, and to conduct scientific excavations of such Neolithic sites as Karup in Qamdo, Chokong in Lhasa and Trango in Shannan. Protection repair measures were adopted for the ancient architectures and sites like the monasteries of Jokhang, Tashilhunpo, Sakya, Samye, Champa Ling, Shalu and Palkhor Chode, the Mount Dzong (Dzongri) Anti-British Monument in Gyangze County, and the Norbulingka. In particular, from 1989 to 1994, the state allocated 55 million yuan and a great amount of gold, silver and other precious materials for the renovation of the Potala Palace. In 2001 a special fund of 380 million yuan was apportioned to repair the Potala Palace, Norbulingka and Sakya Monastery. In the period

2006-2010, the central government allocated 570 million yuan for the repair and protection of 22 key cultural relics sites in Tibet. Such a colossal investment and large-scale renovation were unprecedented in China's history of cultural relics protection.

Notes:

[1] See *Tibet Daily*, June 11, 2007, p. 2.

[2] See *Tibet Daily*, October 15 and 28, 2008, p. 2 and p.1.

94. What is the situation of Tibetan studies? What important achievements have been scored?

The history of Tibetan studies can be dated back to the Sui and Tang dynasties (581-907) or even earlier. Modern research methods were introduced into Tibetan studies in the late 19th and early 20th centuries.

After the People's Republic was founded in 1949 the state created favorable conditions for the development of Tibetology and for the study of Tibetan history, religions, culture, economy, politics and society. To facilitate Tibetan-language teaching and Tibetology in general, the state set up the Institute of Ethnology under the Chinese Academy of Social Sciences, the Central Institute of Nationalities (now Minzu University of China), and various ethnic institutes in Tibet, Qinghai and other places inhabited mainly by ethnic minorities in southwest and northwest China, and dispatched many specialists on Tibetan studies to teach at these institutions. In 1982 the Tibet Academy of Social Sciences was established, and the China Tibetology Research Center set up in 1986 in Beijing.

Today there are some 60 Tibetan studies institutions across China, employing more than 3,000 specialists and assitants of Tibetan and other ethnic groups. A large number of them are undertaking such big research subjects as the *Tibetan-Chinese*

Dictionary, the Tibetan epic *The Legend of King Gesar*, Tibetan medicine and drugs, economic and social development in Tibet and the CPC policies concerning Tibet. They are also engaged in the collation and study of Sanskrit sutras, research into the religions of Tibet, the compilation of *A Comprehensive History of Tibet* and checking the Tibetan version of the Buddhist *Tripitaka*. They have completed more than 300 important projects, published a large number of works on Tibetan studies and collections of Chinese-Tibetan historical documents. Nearly 30 magazines, including the *China Tibetology* and *Tibetan Studies*, are published regularly, with editions in the Tibetan, Chinese and English languages.

Along with the progress in international exchanges since the 1980s, more than 100 academic seminars have been held on topics covering Tibetan history, language, religions, philosophy, literature and art, education, astronomy and calendric system, and Tibetan medicine. Cooperation in these projects has been established with a dozen countries, including the US, Japan, Austria and Germany, and a few hundred scholars from 20 countries and regions and overseas Tibetans have visited China for academic exchanges and research cooperation. Chinese scholars of Tibetan studies have also been invited to lecture or attend academic seminars abroad.

95. What is the situation of Tibetan software application and Internet use in Tibet?

In 1984 a Tibetan-script processing system compatible with Chinese and English versions was developed. In 1997 an international-standard Tibetan character code was approved, making the Tibetan script the first ethnic-minority script in China with an international standard. At present, a Tibetan grammar framework and a grammar system have been set up in Tibet for automatic machine processing, and the work to enable automatic word segmentation and chunking identification for texts in the Tibetan script by machine is under way. A machine-based Tibetan-Chinese dictionary (120,000 entries) has been completed, while an electronic dictionary of Tibetan grammar needed for machine translation has been devised, laying a solid foundation for promoting Tibetan culture in the information age.

The central and local governments have worked hard to promote the development and popularization of the Internet in Tibet. By the end of 2009, some 1,600 Internet websites had been opened in Tibet, ten being news websites, with 530,000 Internet users and an Internet penetration rate of 18.6%.

96. How is Tibetan Thangka art being protected?

Thangka, a Tibetan scroll painting on cloth or silk, is a unique art created by the Tibetan people. There are many varieties that fall generally into two categories: One is embroidery on silk, which can be seen as huge-size works for sunning Buddha on hillside by monasteries on religious festivals, and the other is a painting done on cloth with pigments of gold, red and black. Besides the traditional subjects of religion, the history and current life of the Tibetan people are also depicted. This folk craft is well protected by the central and local authorities.

97. What are the traditional sports in Tibet?

To develop sports programs and improve the people's health was an important policy determined when New China was founded in 1949. With the support of the central government, sports programs have been developing steadily in Tibet, and the physical fitness of the local people have been constantly improved. Now there are more than 1,000 locations for sports activities. The modern gymnasium in the northern suburbs of Lhasa can accommodate 4,000 audiences and people can engage in basketball, volleyball, table-tennis, badminton, martial arts, weight-lifting and wrestling.

Traditional Tibetan sports, such as horse racing, horsemanship, polo, archery, wrestling, two-person tug-of-war, yak racing, and mountaineering, have been incorporated into modern competitions. Along with the great improvement of the region's production and living conditions, the residents' health has also been improved, and traditional sports have more participants than the past in cities and towns as well as in farming and pastoral areas.

98. Is the citizen's right to education ensured in Tibet? Are there any special policies in this regard?

An important part of the work of the central government and the local governments at all levels in Tibet is the development of local education programs and the raise of the cultural level of the Tibetans and other ethnic minorities in the Tibet Autonomous Region, so as to boost the local economic and social progress and to ensure human rights protection for all the people living in Tibet. This has been guaranteed through legislation.

Article 46 of the Chinese Constitution states that "Citizens of the People's Republic of China have the duty as well as the right to receive education." Article 37 of the Law on Regional Ethnic Autonomy states that "The organs of self-government of ethnic autonomous areas shall independently develop education for their local ethnic groups by eliminating illiteracy, setting up various kinds of schools, making available nine-year compulsory education, developing regular senior secondary education and secondary vocational and technical education in various forms, and developing higher education where possible and necessary so as to train specialists from among all the ethnic-minority groups. The organs of self-government of ethnic autonomous areas shall set up public primary schools and secondary schools, mainly boarding schools and schools providing subsidies, in pastoral areas and economically underdeveloped, sparsely-populated mountainous areas inhabited by ethnic-minority groups."

Article 2 of the Compulsory Education Law states that "Compulsory education means education which is uniformly provided by the state and which all the school-age children and adolescents must receive, and constitutes a public welfare undertaking which must be guaranteed by the state." Article 4 states that "All school-age children and adolescents of the nationality of the People's Republic of China shall, in accordance with the law, enjoy the equal right, and fulfill the obligation, to receive compulsory education, regardless of sex, ethnic status or race, family financial conditions, religious belief, etc.".

Before the peaceful liberation of Tibet there was not a single school there in the modern sense, except some old-style private or government-run schools that catered to only 2,000 monks or children of aristocratic families. Less than 2% of Tibet's school-age children had access to school, and the serfs and slaves were totally deprived of the right to education. Today, a fairly complete modern education system has been established in Tibet, and the spread of education has been constantly boosted. By the end of 2009 Tibet had 1,014 schools of various kinds, with an enrollment of 538,426, and 98.8% of the school-age children were in school. To date, six-year compulsory education (primary school) has been implemented in all the 74 counties (county-level cities and districts) of Tibet, nine-year compulsory education (primary and junior high school) has been implemented in 70 counties, the illiteracy rate among young and middle-aged people has been reduced from 95% before the Democratic Reform to below 2.4% now, and 15-year-olds receive 6.3 years of education on average.

The Compulsory Education Law, promulgated and enacted as of April 12, 1986, states that the state implements a system of nine-year compulsory education. With the full support of the state, the children of farmers and herdsmen are all exempted from tuition and textbook fees during the nine-year compulsory education period; boarding students are all exempted from paying board, lodging and tuition fees; and grant-in-aid and scholarship systems are being introduced into primary and high schools in townships and above. In 2005 a total of 220,000 primary and high school students were exempted from paying board, lodging and tuition fees. After the policy was adopted in 1985 the subsidy standards had been raised six times by the end of 2007. The new standards enacted on September 1, 2007 were: in each school year, 1,200 yuan for each primary school student (100 yuan more than in 2006) and 1,350 yuan for each junior high school student in the farming and pastoral areas; and each primary and junior high school student in the border counties and townships would receive 100 yuan more to make the total per capita subsidy 1,300 yuan and 1,450 yuan, respectively. The money all comes from the central government, which appropriated 2,437.2 million yuan for education in 2007 alone. By the end of 2007 a total of 266,000 students in Tibet were provided with free education and accommodation; together with those receiving grant-in-aid, the beneficiary measures reached 420,000 students, which was more than 85% of the total primary and high school students in the farming and pastoral areas.

In addition to the above policies, senior high school graduates in Tibet also enjoy lower college enrollment requirements than those in other parts of the country.

99. What are the school curricula in Tibet?

Besides the Tibetan and Chinese languages, English is also taught in some schools in Tibet. Learning Chinese does not conflict with learning traditional Tibetan culture.

Most primary school classes in Tibet are taught in the Tibetan language. The primary and high schools can choose either of the two teaching modes: in the Tibetan language or in the Chinese language. The primary schools in the farming and herding areas and some high schools choose the first mode, while township primary schools and most high schools choose the second. Either way, Tibetan language class is taught in all schools.

Six local institutes of higher learning teach 90 subjects in 11 categories, including philosophy, economics and law, and confer master's degrees in 18 subjects, including Tibetan medicine, Tibetan pharmacology, Tibetan language and Tibetan history. The Tibetan language is a required course for all students.

100. Is there any limit on the learning and use of the Tibetan language? How is the Tibetan language used in Tibet?

The Chinese Constitution states that "All ethnic groups have the freedom to use and develop their own spoken and written languages." Over the past 50 years governments at all levels have implemented in accordance with the law the central government stipulated on protecting and developing the Tibetan language and script, and made energetic efforts to promote the learning and use of the Tibetan language.

Both the Tibetan and Chinese languages are given equal importance in Tibet, with priority given to the former. Both languages are used for all laws and regulations, resolutions and other formal documents, newspapers and periodicals, radio and television programs in Tibet, and the Tibetan language is used for all mass rallies. The Tibetan language is one of the ethnic-minority languages used on important occasions by the National People's Congress and the National Committee of the Chinese People's Political Consultative Conference.

Of the books published in Tibet, 70% are in the Tibetan language. Fourteen Tibetan-language magazines such as the *Tibetan Literature and Arts*, *Spang-rgyan-me-tog*, *Tibetan Culture*, and a dozen Tibetan language newspapers such as *People's*

Daily (Tibetan edition), *Tibet Daily* and *Lhasa Evening News* are circulated across the region. The Tibetan language is a major subject for students in all schools. When recruiting workers and cadres and enrolling students, the Tibetan-language users enjoy preferential treatment. Both the Tibetan and Chinese languages are used for all the names of workplaces, as well as street signs and public facilities.

In 1995 the Tibetan Language Standardization Committee was set up in Tibet in charge of the standardization and regulation work of the language. The international standard Tibetan character code has been approved by the International Organization for Standardization, making Tibetan script the first ethnic-minority script in China with an international standard.

101. What is the situation of modern education in Tibet? What are the local school enrollment and illiteracy rates?

An important part of the work of the central government and the governments at all levels in Tibet is to develop local education programs and raise the cultural level of the Tibetans and other ethnic minorities so as to boost local economic and social development and ensure that the Tibetans fully enjoy human rights. Since the peaceful liberation, Tibet has seen unprecedented progress in its educational programs.

Before 1951 there was not a single school in the modern sense, except some old-style private or government-run schools that only catered to 2,000 monks or children of the nobility. Less than 2% of school-age children had access to education, the illiteracy rate among ordinary people was as high as 95%, and the serfs and slaves were completely deprived of the right to education.

Today, a fairly complete modern education system has been established in Tibet, covering preschool, elementary, special, vocational, higher and adult education. There are six institutes of higher learning, 118 high schools, six secondary vocational schools, 884 primary schools and 819 teaching centers, with a combined enrollment of 538,426. The right to education for the people of the autonomous region, most of whom are Tibetans, is guaranteed, and their knowledge of science and culture has been greatly increased. By 2009 all counties (cities and districts) had instituted nine-year compulsory education, the minimum schooling was 6.3 years, 98.8% of primary-school-age children were at school, and the illiteracy rate among adults had dropped to below 2.4%.

102. How much money has the central government put into education in Tibet?

Since the peaceful liberation the state has adopted vigorous measures to develop education in Tibet. From 1952 to 2007 the state financial input into Tibet totaled 22.562 billion yuan, of which 13.989 billion yuan was paid in the period 2002-2007. Provinces and municipalities in other parts of China also rendered energetic support for the development of education in Tibet in terms of manpower, materials and finance. So far, more than 7,000 teachers have been sent from other parts of China to aid Tibet in this respect.

Since 1985 the state has covered all tuition as well as food and boarding expenses for compulsory-education students from Tibet's agricultural and pastoral families. In 2007 the state decided to exempt all primary and junior high school students of all tuition and other fees, thus making Tibet the first area in China to enjoy free compulsory education.

In recent years the state has increased its investment in improving school facilities and learning conditions, spending 1.85 billion yuan between 2000 and 2006 on renovating old school buildings and constructing new ones, totaling 1.5 million sq m in floor space. From 2004 to 2007 a total of 133 classrooms equipped with computers were built, in addition to 983 distance-education locations served by satellites and 1,763 educational-resource systems. As a result, most of Tibet's primary and high schools possess hi-tech teaching facilities.

Tibet has already formed a relatively comprehensive education system ranging from preschool education and nine-year compulsory education to secondary education, higher education, vocational education, distance education, correspondence education and special education.

103. How many college graduates does Tibet have, and what is their employment situation?

Tibet set up its first institute of higher learning in 1965. By the end of 2009 some 46,413 people had graduated from various institutes of higher learning in Tibet, and had 30,264 students on campus. Secondary schools had graduated 526,783 students by the end of 2009. Nearly 20,000 cadres had received relevant training and nearly 10,000 had received diplomas from colleges and secondary schools. Many of these people are playing backbone roles as leaders, specialists and technicians.

104. What college subjects in Tibet confer master's and doctoral degrees?

In 2006 Tibet gained the right to confer master's degrees in 18 subjects from the Office of the State Council Academic Degrees Committee. The Tibet University offered 12 subjects: Tibetan language and literature (2 subjects), Tibetan history, Tibetan fine arts, music, public service management, education, crop cultivation, ecology, water conservancy and hydropower, preventive veterinary medicine and silviculture. The Tibet Nationalities University had six subjects: ethnic studies, economy of ethnic minorities, Chinese philosophy (focusing on Tibetan religion), classical Chinese literature, arts, and special history. The Tibetan Traditional Medical College had one subject.

In 1998 The Tibet University was empowered by the Ministry of Education to confer master's degrees, and began to recruit postgraduates the following year. The Tibet Nationalities University obtained the authorization in 2003, and began its postgraduate enrollment in 2004.

The Tibetan Traditional Medical College began to enroll its first batch of postgraduates in 1999. In 2004 the college began to enroll, jointly with the Beijing University of Traditional Chinese Medicine, doctoral students.

The Postgraduate School under the Chinese Academy of

Agricultural Science opened its Tibet branch in October 2008. Its first batch of postgraduates numbered 46, for three-year courses.

The Tibet University is currently applying to confer doctorates in Tibetan language and literature, and Tibetan history.

105. How are classes for Tibetans run outside Tibet? Will that interfere with the students' heritage of their native culture?

Starting in 1985, the central government has allocated special funds to run classes for Tibetans in relatively developed cities and provinces. They mainly recruit students from farming and herding areas in Tibet. The tuition and lodging fees are borne by the cities and provinces concerned. These cities and provinces have adopted preferential policies in terms of finance and personnel, and are constantly improving their teaching conditions.

Today, 28 schools in 20 provinces and municipalities directly under the central government conduct classes for Tibetan students, as do 58 key senior high schools and 120 colleges and universities in the inland areas. The number of Tibetan students studying in such classes or secondary technical schools totals 21,800, and these institutions have become important training bases for personnel for the Tibet Autonomous Region.

Practice over the past two decades shows that attending classes outside Tibet does not prevent Tibetan students from carrying on the fine traditional Tibetan culture. On the contrary, it has broadened their views and helped them better understand, learn and carry on their traditions.

106. How about the medical and healthcare services in Tibet? What changes have taken place regarding the average lifespan and infant mortality rate? What has the government done to improve the local people's health?

Before the peaceful liberation, there were only three official medical organs and a small number of private clinics in Tibet, with fewer than 100 employees. Together with other Tibetan medicine practitioners serving the people, the total number of doctors would have been around 400. But thanks to the support of the central government and the whole country, and after more than 50 years of efforts, Tibet has established a medical and healthcare network, combining the Tibetan, Western and traditional Chinese medicines, centered on Lhasa and covering cities and townships in the entire region. By 2009 there were 1,329 medical and health institutions, with 8,553 hospital beds and 10,047 medical workers, which meant 2.95 beds and 3.47 medical workers for every 1,000 patients. The medical service system, based on free medical treatment, covers all farmers and herders, who have been eligible for 140 yuan of free medical service since 2009, compared with 40 yuan in 2004. As a result of the improvement in medical services, the average life span in Tibet has been extended from 35.5 years in the 1950s to 67 years at present, and the population increased from 1.1409 million in 1951 to 2.9003 million by the end of 2009, 95% of whom were Tibetans and people of other ethnic minorities.

Before the peaceful liberation, the average life span of the Tibetans was 35.5 years, the mortality rate 28‰, and that of infants 430‰.

In the old days, the Tibetans were harassed by rampant malignant epidemics. It was recorded that during the 150 years before the peaceful liberation, the region was stricken by smallpox four times and typhoid twice (in 1934 and 1937). Since the peaceful liberation the central government and the local governments at all levels have energetically developed local medical and healthcare services. Since the 1960s smallpox has been eradicated in Tibet, and some other malignant diseases have been either eradicated or put under control. Government-subsidized immunization efforts have reached 80% of local children.

The state has implemented a policy of free medical service in the farming and pastoral areas of Tibet, and the amount of fee exemption is being constantly raised. In 2006 the government allocated 21 million yuan to upgrade the medical equipment in most prefectures (cities), and 205 million yuan to subsidize medical services by 90 yuan per person annually, which was further increased to 100 yuan in 2007 and 140 yuan in 2008. A total of 2.398 million farmers and herders have joined the cooperative medical service. The medical expenses of urban employees are borne by their employers. Urban medical insurance was introduced in 2007, covering all city dwellers by the end of that year. In addition, Tibet has joined a national program aimed at raising the awareness of millions of farmers of taking care of their health. The state planned to earmark 70 million yuan in 2009 for an emergency medicine reserve, fund for unexpected incidents of public health, training of medical workers in the farming and pastoral areas, immunization, and prevention and treatment of endemic diseases.[1]

Note:

[1] See "Tibet Speeds Up Social Welfare Projects", *People's Daily*, December 7, 2008, p. 4.

107. What has the government done to protect and develop Tibetan medicine? What is the state of the industrialization of Tibetan medicine and pharmacology?

Tibetan medicine has distinct characteristics and is an important component of China's medicinal tradition. During its long history of development, Tibetan medicine has absorbed the essence of traditional Chinese medicine practiced in inland regions, as well as that of the ancient Indian and Arabic medicines. But the extremely backward feudal serfdom in the old times in Tibet hampered its development. At the time of the Democratic Reform in 1959 Tibet had only three small official medical bodies: the "Chakpori Zhopanling" (Medicine King Hill Institute for Saving All Living Beings) in Lhasa, the "Mantsikhang" (Institute of Tibetan Medicine and Astrology) and the Hall of Gathering Immortals in Shigatse, with a total of less than 100 medial students and only 20 at "Chakpori Zhopanling." In addition, there were a few folk Tibetan doctors and some monasteries also taught medicine, providing medical service only for high officials, senior monks, religious officials and nobles, while the vast number of peasants and herders could not afford any medical treatment. Many places had no hospital, no doctor and no medicine at all.

Since the Democratic Reform in 1959, the central government has attached great importance to the research into and development of Tibetan medicine and drugs. In 1986 and 1996 two meetings were held respectively in Tibet to clarify the guidelines and goals for the development of Tibetan medicine and drugs in the new era.

A number of works on Tibetan medicine and drugs have been published, including the *Four Medical Classics*, *80 Colorful Hanging Charts of the Four Medical Classics on Thangka, China Medical Encyclopedia · Tibetan Medicine, Tibetan Herbal Medicine, A Dictionary of Tibetan Herbal Medicine, Tibetan Astronomy and Calendar, Tibetan Medicine Diagnostics, A Dictionary of Chinese Herbal Medicine in Tibet, A New Compendium of Tibetan Medicine, Tibetan Medicine and Prescriptions, A Dictionary of Tibetan Medicine and Drugs*, and *A Detailed Explanation of the Four Medical Classics*.

In 1959 the "Chakpori Zhopanling" and the "Mantsikhang" were merged into the Lhasa Hospital of Tibetan Medicine, which also began to train personnel. By 1970 it had trained nearly 100 pharmacists of Tibetan medicine. In 1974 a course in Tibetan medicine was opened at the Lhasa Medical School, marking the establishment of formal training in Tibetan medicine. In 1983 the regional Tibetan Medical School was founded; in 1985 the Tibet University set up its Tibetan Medicine Department and began to enroll students; in 1989 this Tibetan Medicine Department and the Tibetan Medical School were merged into the Traditional Tibetan Medical College, which enrolled its first batch of postgraduates in 1999. In 2004 the college began to enroll, jointly with the Beijing University of Traditional Chinese Medicine, doctoral students in traditional Tibetan medicine, thus forming a complete educational system in Tibetan medicine. By 2007, the college had trained 1,256 people in Tibetan medicine.

Tibetan medical organs and research institutions have been set up across the entire region. Today, there is one regional hospital, six prefecture hospitals, and 10 county hospitals, with a total of 64 departments in Tibetan medicine, and one regional research institute of Tibetan medicine, one institute under the Traditional Tibetan Medical College, and one research office each in Ngari, Shigatse, Shannan, Nagchu and Chamdo prefectures. There are 1,850 Tibetan medical professionals, treating nearly one million outpatients each year, and more than 100 specialists in Tibetan medicine, in addition to 600 village doctors.

Since the 10th Five-year Plan period (2001-2005), Tibetan medicine has been listed as one of the three pillar industries to be energetically developed and supported in Tibet. By the end of 2007 a total of 18 Tibetan pharmaceutical factories had been approved for operation. They employed 1,400 workers and produced 804.5 tons of Tibetan medicines in 360 categories every year, with an output value of nearly 662 million yuan.[1] In the first seven months of 2008, the Pharmaceuticals Factory of Traditional Tibetan Medicine in Lhasa produced 41.33 tons of Tibetan medicines, with an output value of 74 million yuan, an increase of 59% year on year.[2] There are also some local hospitals producing Tibetan drugs.

The Hospital of Tibetan Medicine was opened in Beijing, which also acts as an introducer of Tibetan medicine to the world. In 2005 the China Tibetology Research Center set up the Institute for Tibetan Medicine Studies for better research, development, use and spread of Tibetan medicine.

Notes:

[1] See the *Chinese Tibetan Culture: Collection of Papers of the Kathmandu Forum.*

[2] See *Tibet Daily*, August 27, 2008, p. 5.

Protection of the Ecological Environment

VIII

108. What is the current situation of the ecological environment in Tibet? What measures have been adopted by the Chinese government to protect the ecological environment there? How many nature reserves are there in Tibet?

The Chinese government has established the rational development and utilization of natural resources and the protection of ecological environment as its basic national policy. The central government and the local government of Tibet attach great importance to environmental protection in Tibet. The central government chose Tibet as an important national standard for ecological security at its Fifth Forum on the Work in Tibet in 2010, and set maintaining a good ecological environment as one of the major goals of local development. In February 2009 the State Council passed the Plan for the Protection and Construction of Ecological Security in Tibet (2008-2030), which involves an investment of 15.5 billion yuan to implement ten projects of ecological improvement and environmental protection there.

The Tibet Autonomous Region aims to develop production to enrich the people while maintaining a good ecological environment, adhering to the development road with Chinese and Tibetan characteristics, and including the good ecological environment and eco-friendly construction in its development plan. Special environmental-protection organs have been established in the autonomous region, all its prefecture-level cities and most counties. The local government of Tibet has enacted and implemented relevant local regulations and administrative rules including the Regulations for the Environmental Protection in the Tibet Autonomous Region, Regulations for Forest Protection in the Tibet Autonomous Region, and Temporary Measures for the Administration of Grasslands in the Tibet Autonomous Region; implemented projects to protect natural forests, reforest farmlands, reduce farming on grasslands, protect and construct natural grasslands, build permanent settlements for herdsmen, promote man-made grasslands and improve existing grasslands; launched a state compensation fund for the loss in forest ecological development and actively carried out the work in desertification prevention and control, soil erosion control, comprehensive harnessing of minor river valleys and the prevention of geological disasters. Meanwhile, Tibet has strengthened its environmental law-enforcement supervision over resource exploitation such as minerals, water, tourism and Tibetan medicine, and the construction of key infrastructure. The mining of gold and iron ore has also been banned throughout the region.

At present, there are 47 nature reserves of various types in Tibet, covering a total area of 413,700 sq km, which accounts for 34.47% of the total area of the region, ranking first in the country. In addition, 21 ecological functional reserves (with one at national level), eight national forest parks, four national geoparks, three national wetland parks and three national scenic zones have been set up.

In order to restore the natural ecosystem, human activities such as economic development are strictly limited in the established nature reserves. As a result, the ecological environment in most of the nature reserves has become stable and is developing in a fine circle. Breeding grounds, habitats and important ecosystems for rare and endangered species, important wetlands for migratory birds, as well as natural landscapes, geological sites and biological sites of scientific importance are now well protected. Jimmy Carter, the former US president, made the following comment on the construction of nature reserves in Tibet: The Tibetans have reserved 40% of their territory to protect endangered species, including snow leopards, wild yaks, Tibetan antelopes and elks.

In today's Tibet, the ecological environment has been basically kept in a primordial state. No major environmental pollution accident has occurred in Tibet, nor has the phenomenon of acid rain. Water and the atmosphere in Tibet are basically unpolluted. It is one of the places with the best environmental quality in the world.

Reference:

Mount Qomolangma Nature Reserve. In order to protect the unique ecosystem there, the Mount Qomolangma Nature Reserve was officially set up on March 18, 1989. As a comprehensive nature reserve, the Mount Qomolangma Nature Reserve aims to protect the whole ecosystem in the area. In 1994 it was designated by the State Council as a national-level nature reserve.

Lhalu Wetland Nature Reserve. The Lhalu Wetland is located near Lhasa, capital of the Tibet Autonomous Region. With an elevation of 3,645 m, it covers an area of 12.2 sq km, and 6.63 sq km of which are its core area. The Lhalu Wetland Nature Reserve is the highest and largest urban natural wetland in China. In order to better protect the wetland, the Lhasa municipal government issued the Measures for the Administration of the Lhalu Wetland Nature Reserve in April 2000, providing guidelines for the protection and administration of the Lhalu Wetland. In 2002 the Lhasa municipal government established the Lhalu Wetland Management Station. On July 23, 2005 it was upgraded to a national-level nature reserve by the State Council.

Changtang Nature Reserve. Located in Nagqu Prefecture and Ngari Prefecture, the Changtang Nature Reserve has a total area of 29.8 million hectares, making it the largest nature reserve in China, and the second in size only to the Northeast Greenland National Park in the world. In 1993 the Changtang Nature Reserve was set up by the People's Government of the Tibet Autonomous Region. In 2000 it was upgraded to a national-level nature reserve by the State Council. It provides protection for the plateau ecosystem, wild animals and endangered species.

109. Will Tibet's environment be damaged by the region's rapid economic development?

China's western development strategy will not destroy Tibet's natural resources and environment. Different from traditional regional development, it not only aims to develop natural resources, but also to uphold sustainable development and promote the coordinated development of population, resources, the environment and the economy in the western regions of China through inputs of capital, technology and personnel.

From the perspective of attaining sustainable development, the local government of Tibet has put ecological improvement and environmental protection at the core of its western development strategy, drawn up a series of plans for eco-environmental improvement, and expressly stipulated that tourism and green agriculture be developed as pillar industries for promoting economic growth in Tibet.

In the implementation of these plans, based on the requirements of optimized development, major development, restricted development and prohibited development, the local government of Tibet is steadily promoting ecological protection, key resource development zones and ecologically sound regions, enhancing ecological engineering projects such as turning farmland to forests and pasture land, closing hillsides to facilitate afforestation in ecologically fragile areas, and energetically carrying out projects for ecological security on the Tibetan Plateau. Meanwhile, no major construction projects may be authorized until an evaluation of their impact on the environment has been conducted first. Moreover, once they are authorized, investment must include the expenses of environmental protection and pollution control.

It is therefore clear that China's western development program will not damage Tibet's natural resources and environment. On the contrary, it should be conducive to their protection.

110. Tibet has a fragile plateau ecosystem. What measures have been taken by the Tibet Autonomous Region to control environmental pollution? What rules and regulations concerning environmental protection have been implemented?

In order to reduce the adverse effects caused to the ecological environment by industrial development, the government of the Tibet Autonomous Region adheres to the principle of placing equal emphasis on both industrial development and environmental protection. As industries are developed in the region, Tibet makes every effort to ensure that while they bring about economic profits they produce social and environmental benefits as well. No industrial project is to be launched just because of its envisaged economic benefit or just because it will fill a gap in the field. The government has adopted a series of pollution-prevention measures to ensure that the development of modern industry does not damage the ecological environment. First, industrial pollution is dealt with through industrial restructuring, product-mix adjustment and technological transformation. For instance, the Lhasa Leather Factory has imported environmental-protection facilities along with advanced technologies and equipment from Germany. The Lhasa Brewery, which used to be a big polluter, has spent more than four million yuan on equipment to treat industrial sewage as part of its technological transformation efforts. As a result, its sewage discharge now meets the specified standard. Second, more strict supervision and management of the environment have been implemented. Rectification has been carried out in respect of enterprises that fail to meet the requirements for pollutant discharge. In accordance with the guiding principle of "opening big enterprises and shutting down small ones" for industrial restructuring, six vertical-kiln cement production lines in Lhasa which used to be serious polluters have been shut down. Enterprises causing serious pollution are banned, as are outdated technologies and equipment prohibited by the State.

Tibet implements the Regulations for Environmental Protection in the Tibet Autonomous Region and Measures for the Administration of Mineral Resources in the Tibet Autonomous Region, as well as related measures and detailed rules for the implementation of the Land Administration Law of the People's Republic of China, Water Law of the People's Republic of China, Law of the People's Republic of China on Water and Soil Conservation, Grassland Law of the People's Republic of China and Law of the People's Republic of China on the Protection of Wildlife. An effective supervision and management system for environmental protection and pollution control is now in place.

111. Some people say that China's western development drive will lead to large-scale colonization of Tibet and destroy the ecological environment there. Is that true?

The central government and the local government of Tibet attach great importance to the coordinated development of the economy and the environment in Tibet. In recent years, more money has been invested to the ecological improvement in Tibet. From the perspective of attaining sustainable development in the region, the local government of Tibet has expressly stipulated that tourism[1] and green agriculture be developed as the pillar industries for promoting economic growth in Tibet, and drawn up a series of plans for eco-environmental improvement. As a result, Tibet boasts rapid economic and social development while its ecological environment is still in a pristine state.

China's western development strategy will not destroy Tibet's natural resources and environment. It is a long-term systematic project implemented by the Chinese government. Different from traditional regional exploitation, it not only aims to develop natural resources, but also to uphold sustainable development and promote the coordinated development of population, resources, environment and economy in the country's western regions through inputs of capital, technology and personnel. As for each project, full consideration shall be given to the protection and improvement of the local environment, from initiation to implementation and yielding of returns. Therefore, the Chinese government has put ecological improvement and environmental protection at the core of its western development strategy. Measures have been taken to strengthen the evaluation system of environmental impact and implement an environmental supervision system for projects; promote ecological projects, including returning farmland to forests and pasture, and closing hillsides to facilitate afforestation in ecologically fragile areas. Tibet is still the "source of rivers" and "ecological source" for the areas in South China, South Asia and Southeast Asia. Hence, the claim that "China's western development will lead to large-scale colonization of Tibet and destroy the ecological environment there" is utterly groundless.

Note:

[1] According to the tourism development plan and goal drawn up by the Tibet Autonomous Region, by 2010 Tibet had played host to six million domestic and foreign tourists, its earnings from tourism totaling six billion yuan. And by 2015 it will play host to nine million domestic and foreign tourists, and its earnings from tourism will total 11.6 billion yuan, accounting for 15% of the total revenue of the region. See also *Tibet Creates Destination Image of "Roof of the World, Mystical Tibet"* published on October 26, 2008 in the *Tibet Daily*.

112. Some people claim that the Chinese government has been destroying Tibet's environment by conducting nuclear tests in Tibet, pumping out water from the Holy Lake to build a hydropower station, felling large numbers of trees, etc. Is that true?

It is true that Tibet's ecological environment is facing challenges, for example, the deteriorating quality of grassland and threats to some rare wildlife species. On the whole, however, Tibet's ecological environment is being basically kept in a primordial state. No major environmental pollution accident has occurred in Tibet, nor has the phenomenon of acid rain appeared. The water and air in Tibet are basically unpolluted. So far, it is still one of the places with the best environmental quality in the world.

According to data gathered by environmental protection departments over many years, the natural radiation level in Tibet satisfies the standard stipulated by national regulations for radiation protection. It is worth noting that some people in other countries have accused the Chinese government of conducting nuclear tests, dumping nuclear waste and producing nuclear pollution in Tibet, which are utterly groundless. The Chinese government has never conducted any nuclear test in Tibet. And the charge of dumping nuclear waste is sheer nonsense.

All major projects in Tibet have to include eco-environmental protection as a key task in resources development. With
respect to the hydropower station at Yamzhoyumco Lake, full
consideration was given to the protection of the ecological environment, starting from the decision to build the station to its
design and construction. Since this hydropower station was put
into operation, electricity generation has not caused the water
level in the lake to drop, which would have harmed the natural
eco-environment of the lake. Meanwhile, Tibet has been active
in afforestation, forest protection and fire prevention, sealing off
mountainous areas to facilitate afforestation and fighting against
indiscriminate felling of trees. Since the 1960s more then 70
million trees have been planted, and 140,000 hectares of mountainous areas have been sealed off annually for afforestation.
There is now 14.6265 million hectares of forest in Tibet. The
forested area is expanding every year, with the increase of standing timber greater than that of felled timber.

113. What positive efforts have been made by the Tibet Autonomous Region to protect biodiversity and rare animals?

Tibet is still one of the best areas in the world as far as the ecological environment is concerned. The complex terrain and varied climate there have produced rich biological resources. There are now over 6,400 vascular plants in Tibet, 39 of which are under special State protection as rare and endangered species. There are 798 species of wild vertebrates, 125 of which are under special State protection, accounting for more than one third of the total number of wild animals in China under special State protection. There are 45 species of rare animals endemic to China in Tibet, including the Tibetan antelope, Tibetan wild donkey, wild yak, Bengal tiger, black-necked crane, clouded leopard and snow leopard. In order to effectively protect the region's biodiversity and safeguard the sustained utilization of biological resources and the benign circle of the ecosystem, 47 nature reserves of various types have been set up in Tibet, covering a total area of 413,700 sq km and accounting for 34.47% of the total area of the region.

The central government and the People's Government of the Tibet Autonomous Region attach great importance to the protection of the Tibetan antelope, which is categorized by the State as a Class A wild animal to be protected. The hunting of the Tibetan antelope is strictly prohibited. In the early 1990s the Tibet Autonomous Region established a nature reserve in Changtang in northern Tibet, which is the main habitat of the Tibetan antelope. In 2000 it was upgraded to a national-level nature reserve. The Tibet Autonomous Region has set up an administration, sub-administrations and administrative stations in the Changtang Nature Reserve and other habitats of the Tibetan antelope, expanded forestry organs and staff, and strengthened law enforcement and publicity of the relevant laws, ruthlessly cracking down on the hunting of Tibetan antelopes. Tibet has established a cooperation system with Qinghai Province and the Xinjiang Uygur Autonomous Region for the protection of the Tibetan antelope. In addition, joining hands with the Worldwide Fund for Nature and other related international authorities, China has put forward the Guidelines for the Protection of the Tibetan Antelope, calling on related countries and people to crack down on the poaching of Tibetan antelopes and the smuggling of Tibetan antelope products.

Through the efforts in the past decade, great achievements have been made in the protection of the Tibetan antelope. The number of these animals in Tibet has jumped to 150,000 from the figure of 50,000-70,000 in 1995.

114. Has the construction of the Qinghai-Tibet Railway produced any impact on the environment along the railway line?

Making the Qinghai-Tibet Railway an eco-friendly railway line was the goal set at the time the project was appraised. In order to protect the ecological environment alongside it, the builders spent 1.54 billion yuan on environmental-protection facilities, a record sum in this aspect for rail construction in China. During the construction the builders took a series of strict measures to protect the environment, which achieved remarkable success. For example, they established 33 passageways for migrating wild creatures at different sections of the line, and implemented all possible measures to keep the permafrost stable and protect wetlands. The construction of the Qinghai-Tibet Railway has produced little adverse impact on the ecological environment of the Qinghai-Tibet Plateau.

Since the Qinghai-Tibet Railway was opened to traffic on July 1, 2006, related departments have made plans to protect the natural environment along the railway line, strictly enforced laws and regulations concerning environmental protection, and taken powerful measures to protect the local ecosystem. The stations along the Golmud-Lhasa section of the Qinghai-Tibet Railway all use environment-friendly energy sources such as electricity, solar energy and wind energy for heating. All the passenger trains leaving or entering Tibet are equipped with sewage and rubbish collection devices. Garbage from the trains is collected by vacuum sewage suction trucks at Golmud and Lhasa stations for central treatment, thus ensuring zero discharge of sewage and waste along the railway line. Wherever possible, remote automatic control and mechanized maintenance are adopted to reduce the number of both operation organs and their staff on the plateau. According to environmental monitoring data, no adverse impact has been produced on the ecological environment along the Qinghai-Tibet Railway since it was opened to traffic.

In July, 2008, the Golmud-Lhasa section of the Qinghai-Tibet Railway won the title of "National Environment-friendly Project," which is the highest honor given to a construction project in China as far as environmental protection is concerned.

115. What measures have been taken by the Tibet Autonomous Region to deal with garbage treatment in urban areas?

The Tibet Autonomous Region has all along attached great importance to the protection of the urban environment, brought it into urban master planning for development, and boosted investment in environmental improvement in urban areas. By 2009 Tibet had spent 300 million yuan to build garbage disposal plants in Lhasa and six prefecture seats. In March, 2005, the Lhasa municipal government issued the Measures for the Prohibition of the Production, Sale and Use of Disposable Tableware and Plastic Bags, targeting at "white pollution" first. The elimination of plastic bags is well under way in the autonomous region, greatly contributing to the comprehensive clean-up of the urban environment.

During the Twelfth Five-Year Plan period Tibet will build 61 garbage treatment plants at seven prefecture seats, county seats, and major border cities and towns.

116. Will the development of tourism affect environmental protection in Tibet?

Developing specialty industries with relatively little impact on the ecological environment has always been an important policy measure in accelerating the economic development of Tibet. The central government proclaimed that it would build Tibet into "the world's most important tourist destination" at its Fifth Forum on Work in Tibet, held in 2010. Tibet is developing tourism in spite of the extremely fragile local ecosystem, and regards tourism as one of its pillar industries, which fully demonstrates that the central government and the local government of Tibet attach great importance to the protection of the ecological system.

The Tibet Autonomous Region adheres to the "principle of sustainable development" in the development of tourism, places great emphasis on the coordination between tourism development and the protection of the environment and the cultural heritage, and properly handles the relationship between the exploitation of tourism resources and environmental protection. It promotes uniform planning, scientific exploitation, effective protection and sustainable usage to attain the organic integration of economic, social and ecological benefits.

117. It is said that forests have been cut down on a large scale in Tibet. Is this true?

Tibet boasts 14.6265 million hectares of forest, with a forest coverage rate of 11.91%, over 98% of which is natural and primitive forest. Most forest resources are kept in a primordial state, although some along transport arteries have been cut down or burnt by fire.

Since 2000 the Tibet Autonomous Region has implemented several projects to protect natural forest resources and restore farmland to forest, and set up a state compensation fund to benefit the forest ecology, giving effective protection to the natural forests in Tibet.

118. Tibet has witnessed the snowline rising and glaciers melting in recent years. Were they caused by economic over-exploitation of Tibet?

In recent years, due to the impact of factors such as global warming and the aridity of the Qinghai-Tibet Plateau, many regions in the world have encountered environmental problems including snowlines retreating and glaciers melting. This is a global issue confronting the whole mankind. In fact, with a population of only 2.9003 million, Tibet has an extremely limited impact on this issue. Nevertheless, the Central Government and the local government of Tibet have placed great emphasis on alleviating it.

Conforming to the requirements of the Scientific Outlook on Development, the Tibet Autonomous Region is energetically transforming its ideas of development, innovating development patterns and enhancing development quality. It will gradually form resource-conserving modes of growth and consumption, and follow a road of sustainable development when developing production to enrich the people while maintaining a sound ecological environment. At the same time, we appeal to the whole world for further international cooperation to solve the environmental problems that challenge human society.

119. What has been the impacts of global warming on economic and social development in Tibet?

Climate change is now a major challenge confronting mankind. Located on the Qinghai-Tibet Plateau, Tibet has a peculiar natural environment and geographical location, which make it particularly vulnerable to the effects of global warming. But it is worth noticing that, with a small population, Tibet is limited in production scale and consumption level, contributing very little to global warming.

The central government and the local government of Tibet place great emphasis on coping with climate change. They have adopted powerful measures to enhance the ability to deal with climate change, energetically making contributions to the fight against global warming. In recent years, Tibet has speeded up the development of clean energy sources, including solar energy and methane. A new pattern featuring the comprehensive utilization of solar, geothermal, wind and micro-hydro energies has taken shape. The local government of Tibet has implemented a series of plans to strengthen environmental protection, continuously increased forest coverage, and effectively enhanced the carbon sequestration of the ecosystem. Especially in February 2009, the State Council adopted the Planning for the Protection and Construction of an Ecological Security Barrier in Tibet

(2008-2030), which plans to spend 15.5 billion yuan by 2030 to implement ten ecological-improvement and environmental-protection projects, and basically build the Tibet ecological security barrier. The central government held the Fifth Forum on Work in Tibet in 2010, designating "maintaining a sound ecological environment in Tibet" as a key strategic task and deciding to "attach more importance to the protection of the ecological environment on the plateau" and "make Tibet an important barrier for ecological security." All these will surely promote the coordinated development of Tibet's ecosystem, economy and society, and make significant contributions to the fight against global warming.

Questions Concerning the Dalai Lama

IX

120. How is the 14th Dalai Lama involved in "Tibet independence"?

In 1653 Qing Dynasty Emperor Shunzhi officially conferred the title of Dalai Lama on the head of the Yellow Sect and established his supreme political and religious status in Tibet. From then on, it became an established rule that each Dalai Lama's accession to the throne had to be authorized by the central government, so as to establish the Dalai Lama's lawful authority over Tibet. The 14th Dalai Lama, now in exile, was authorized to come to the throne by the president of the then Nationalist Government of China in 1940.

After the Opium Wars, beginning in the 1840s, China was gradually reduced to the status of a semi-colonial country. The imperial powers seized opportunities for invasion, and conspired to carve up China, with Tibet included. They plotted "Tibet independence" to split Tibet from China. This was strongly opposed by the Chinese government and people, and thus failed. After the founding of the People's Republic of China in 1949 the central government and the local government of Tibet signed the Agreement on Measures for the Peaceful Liberation of Tibet in 1951, evicted the remnants of the imperial powers from Tibet, and achieved the region's peaceful liberation. In 1959 some reactionary forces among the ruling class in Tibet bent on retaining feudal serfdom colluded with foreign anti-China forces and launched an armed rebellion to split Tibet from China. After failed, the 14th Dalai Lama and his followers fled abroad, founded the so-called "Tibetan government in exile" and engaged in organized political activities to split China.

The Dalai question is by nature a political issue about the Dalai Lama and his followers conspiring to split China and restore theocracy in Tibet. The 14th Dalai Lama has never been a person purely devoted to his religious duties, he has been dabbling in shady politics right up until today.

The constitution of his illegal government in exile explicitly stipulates that the 14th Dalai Lama is the "political and religious leader" of Tibet.

The 14th Dalai Lama claims not to advocate "Tibet independence" but a "middle way," claiming to be seeking "genuine autonomy" for "Greater Tibet." His deceptive political stance denies the fact that Tibet has been an integral part of China since ancient times, and claims that Tibet is a state occupied by China. It opposes the existing social system in Tibet, and wants to create a new one. It envisages the founding of a political entity called "Greater Tibet," that has never actually existed, but would, if realized, cover one quarter of China's total territory. It calls on China to withdraw its troops from Tibet, and build Tibet into an "international peace zone" and a demilitarized zone. It envisages the removal of all non-Tibetans from the so-called

"Greater Tibet" and the setting up of Tibetan embassies in countries throughout the world. From these propositions we can see that the Dalai Lama's political aim is none other than "Tibet independence" and a thorough violation of the Constitution of China.

Moreover, the Dalai clique has long been conducting overseas anti-China activities jeopardizing the modern development of Tibet, and even tried by every means to sabotage the 2008 Beijing Olympics, showing that the Dalai Lama and his clique are engaged in a political conspiracy to split China.

121. What are the central government's basic policies toward the 14th Dalai Lama? Will his request to return to China be accepted?

The central government has kept a constant and clear policy toward the Dalai Lama. It has kept the door to dialogue with the Dalai Lama open so long as he sincerely eschews the claim of "Tibet independence," ceases activities conducted with a view to splitting the country, and openly admits that Tibet is an inalienable part of China, Taiwan is a province of China, and the government of the People's Republic of China is the only legal government representing China.

The central government has never recognized the "Tibetan government in exile." Talks can only be held about the future of the 14th Dalai Lama and his followers with the 14th Dalai Lama himself and his private representatives. Besides, negotiations between the central government and the 14th Dalai Lama are purely internal affairs of China, which needs no foreign mediators and allows no foreign interference.

The 14th Dalai Lama should be viewed from a historical and comprehensive perspective. In the past he was the head of Tibet's feudal system under a theocratic form of government, and was responsible for extra-economic exploitation and inhuman persecution of Tibet's serfs. A few years after the peaceful liberation of Tibet, to maintain the interests of his own family and other feudal serf-owners, he broke the agreement signed with the central government, launched an armed rebellion and fled abroad when the rebellion failed. During his 50 years of exile abroad, the 14th Dalai Lama has betrayed the country by relying on international anti-China forces, conducted activities aimed at splitting China and undermining Tibet's development and stability, and has never done anything good for the Tibetan people.

The 14th Dalai Lama's demand for "more autonomy" and "Greater Tibet," and forcefully pushing the internationalization of the "Tibet Question" are actually part of a two-step separatist strategy — "first autonomy and then independence." In the meantime, the Dalai clique goes even further by continuously creating disturbances to sabotage the stability of Tibet and split China, revealing that the 14th Dalai Lama and his clique have never given up their desire for "Tibet independence."

We hope that the 14th Dalai Lama will truly give up his activities aimed at "Tibet independence" and other conspiracies to restore feudal serfdom, recognize Tibet as an inalienable part of China, stop all his separatist activities and do something beneficial for Tibet's development and its people's well-being.

122. How can the 14th Dalai Lama be regarded as a "defender of human rights," "the Tibetans' spiritual leader," "an honest person" and "an exponent of non-violence" in the eyes of some Westerners?

The 14th Dalai Lama is not a simple religious figure but a political exile long bent on separatist activities undermining national unity. The old Tibet ruled by the Dalai Lama was one of feudal serfdom under a theocracy, a system which was darker and crueler than the European serfdom of the Middle Ages. The Dalai Lama was actually the biggest serf-owner and the theocratic ruler of old Tibet. It is blasphemous to honor the 14th Dalai Lama as a "defender of human rights" and award him a Nobel Peace Prize.

People should review the human rights situation in old Tibet before appraising the 14th Dalai Lama as a "defender of human rights" and "the Tibetans' spiritual leader." Before 1959 Tibet was a dark society of feudal serfdom under a theocracy. Serfs and slaves, accounting for over 95% of Tibet's total population, didn't possess any means of production, and were deprived of personal freedom and political, economic and cultural rights, while serf-owners could abuse, whip, punish, sell, exchange, or even imprison and kill serfs and slaves at will. The 14th Dalai Lama, along with his family, was the biggest serf-owner and the head of this theocracy in old Tibet.

People should also review what the 14th Dalai Lama has done during his over-50 years of exile before honoring him as "an exponent of non-violence." In 1959, in order to maintain the interests of a small number of feudal serf-owners, obstruct the reform of the social system in Tibet, and oppose the emancipation of the Tibetan people, the reactionary upper ruling class of Tibet launched an armed rebellion, which brought disaster to the people of Tibet. After the failed uprising, the Tibetan separatists in exile abroad reorganized their armed forces as "guardians of religion" and a "Special Frontier Force" to conduct destructive activities. Since September 1987, incited and sponsored by the Dalai clique, a small number of separatists in Lhasa have caused many violent incidents aimed at splitting the country, which posed a serious threat to the local people's lives and property. The March 14 riot in 2008 severely sabotaged the sound economic and social development of Tibet and its social order, and caused heavy losses to the broad masses of the people in Tibet. In addition, the Dalai clique oppresses the overseas Tibetans discontented with the Dalai Lama and other Tibetan Buddhist sects by means of threats, attacks and murders. The 14th Dalai Lama can hardly absolve himself from the blame for these violent terrorist activities.

It is to turn a blind eye to the facts to glorify the 14th Dalai Lama as "a defender of human rights," "the spiritual leader of the Tibetans," and "an exponent of non-violence."

123. What about the 14th Dalai Lama's pledge "not to resort to violence"?

The 14th Dalai Lama has repeatedly claimed that he espouses "non-violence." But this is not true. As is known to all, the upper-class reactionary forces in Tibet launched an armed rebellion in 1959. In the guise of nationalism and religion, they resisted the social reform of Tibet, disallowed the Tibetan serfs seeking liberation, and conspired to split the country by relying on foreign forces. The rebellion caused grave disasters to the Tibetan people. The insurgents looted gold and silver, precious Buddhist statues and ritual instruments from monasteries, killed Tibetan cadres, robbed citizens of their property. When the uprising failed, the Tibetan separatists who fled abroad didn't stop their activities aimed at splitting the country. Supported by foreign forces, they reorganized the "guardians of religion" in 1960, and later founded the so-called "Special Frontier Force" composed of several thousand Tibetan exiles. They sent armed mobs and spies to conduct destructive activities in the border areas of Tibet, which severely threatened local Tibetans' lives and property, as well as their normal production and life styles. They also sent a number of trained spies and violent criminals to infiltrate into Tibet for spying, destruction and instigation, and to set up secret reactionary organizations. Since September 1987, incited by the Dalai Lama and supported by foreign anti-

China forces, a small number of separatists have provoked many serious riots in Lhasa, the capital city of the Tibet Autonomous Region. These activities aimed at splitting the country were serious violations of the law. Their terrorist behavior such as beating, smashing, looting, burning and killing threatened the lives and property of the citizens of Lhasa. Concrete evidence proves that the Tibetan separatists in exile abroad not only backed the riots with financial support but also directly plotted, instigated, organized and participated in those terrorist activities. The Dalai clique oppressed overseas Tibetans discontented with their behavior and other Tibetan Buddhist sects by violent means, and sent threatening mails to China. The 14th Dalai Lama can hardly absolve himself from the blame for these terrorist activities. Plenty of facts prove that the 14th Dalai Lama, while pretending to advocate "non-violence," is actually not an exponent of non-violence at all. The fact that he claims that the March 14 violent criminal incident in 2008 was a "peaceful protest" further confirms the truth.

124. What are the contents and nature of the "Five-Point Peace Plan" and the "Seven-Point New Suggestions" made by the 14th Dalai Lama?

During his visit to the United States in 1987, the 14th Dalai Lama delivered a speech called the "Five-Point Peace Plan" to the Human Rights Committee of the US Congress House of Representatives. In June 1988 he held a press conference in the European Parliament Building in Strasbourg, France, and added seven new propositions, briefly called the "Seven-Point New Suggestions."

The main contents of the "Five-Point Peace Plan" are as follows:

1) Transformation of the whole of Tibet into a zone of peace, turning Kham Province in eastern Tibet (Ganzi Prefecture in Sichuan, Diqing Prefecture in Yunnan, Yushu Prefecture in Qinghai and the Qamdo Area of Tibet — *editor's note*) and Amdo Province into a zone of "Ahimsa" (non-violence);

2) Abandonment of China's population-transfer policy which threatens the very existence of the Tibetans as a people;

3) Respect for the Tibetan people's fundamental human rights and democratic freedoms;

4) Restoration and protection of Tibet's natural environment and the abandonment of China's use of Tibet for
the production of nuclear weapons and dumping of
nuclear waste;

5) Commencement of earnest negotiations on the future
status of Tibet and of relations between the Tibetan and
Chinese peoples.

The main contents of the "Seven-Point New Suggestions"
are as follows:

1) The whole of Tibet should become a self-governing
democratic political entity founded on law by the agreement of the people for the common good and the protection of themselves and their environment, in association
with the People's Republic of China. This means that the
Government of Tibet will have the rights to decide on all
affairs relating to Tibet and the Tibetans;

2) The Government of the People's Republic of China could
remain responsible for Tibet's foreign policy. The Government of Tibet should, however, develop and maintain
relations, through its own foreign affairs bureau, in the
field of commerce, education, culture, religion, tourism,
science, sports and other non-political activities. Tibet
should join international organizations concerned with
such activities;

3) The Government of Tibet would seek to ensure this free-

dom by full adherence to the Universal Declaration of Human Rights;

4) The Government should be comprised of a popularly elected Chief Executive, a bicameral legislative branch, and an independent judicial system. Its seat should be in Lhasa;

5) The social and economic system of Tibet should be determined in accordance with the wishes of the Tibetan people;

6) The manufacture, testing, stockpiling of nuclear weapons and other armaments must be prohibited, as well as use of nuclear power and other technologies which produce hazardous waste;

7) A regional peace conference should be called to ensure that Tibet becomes a genuine sanctuary of peace through demilitarization. Until such a peace conference can be convened and demilitarization and neutralization achieved, China could have the right to maintain a restricted number of military installations in Tibet. These must be solely for defense purposes.

The 14th Dalai Lama's "Five-Point Peace Plan" and "Seven-Point New Suggestions" completely violate China's Constitution and laws in the following aspects:

First, the above statements falsify and blur the issue of the sovereignty of Tibet. The preamble to the Constitution of the

People's Republic of China stipulates: "The People's Republic of China is a unitary multi-ethnic state created jointly by the people of all its ethnic groups." Article 4 stipulates: "All ethnic autonomous areas are integral parts of the People's Republic of China." However, the 14th Dalai Lama has long been claiming that "Tibet is an occupied country under colonial rule," and even that "Buddhism spread into China through India along with other important cultures. Therefore, I undoubtedly believe India has more reason than China to claim sovereignty over Tibet." In fact, Tibet has been an inalienable part of China since ancient times. The central government has had indisputable and effective administrative jurisdiction over Tibet since the Yuan Dynasty (1206-1368). The confirmation and installment of the 14th Dalai Lama were also approved by the then Nationalist Government of the Republic of China. The governments of all other countries firmly recognize Tibet as a part of China. This is a common understanding by the international community, as well as the political foundation for China to develop bilateral relations with other countries.

Second, the statements undermine the current political system of Tibet as explicitly stipulated by the Constitution of China. Article 1 of the General Principles in the Constitution of the People's Republic of China stipulates: "The socialist system is the basic system of the People's Republic of China. Disruption of the socialist system by any organization or individual is prohibited." Article 2 stipulates: "All power in the People's Republic of China belongs to the people. The National People's Congress and the local people's congresses at various levels are the organs through which the people exercise state power." The Preface to the Law of the People's Republic of China on Regional Ethnic Autonomy stipulates: "Regional ethnic autonomy is the basic policy adopted by the Communist Party of China for the solution of the ethnic question in China through its application of Marxism-Leninism; it is a basic political system of the State." After the 14th Dalai Lama fled abroad, it was clearly stipulated in his "constitution in exile" that theocracy should be restored in Tibet, and the 14th Dalai Lama, as the political and religious leader, has the right to make the final decisions on all major affairs of the "Tibetan government in exile." The governing body of this exile organization, the so-called "Kalon Tripa," is chosen from among high-ranking lamas. If such a group of people were allowed to rule the people of Tibet, the Dalai clique would restore the theocracy of the old Tibet and once more enslave the Tibetan people.

Third, the so-called "Greater Tibet," which has never existed in history, includes not only the present Tibet Autonomous Region, but also the Tibetan autonomous areas in Sichuan, Qinghai, Gansu and Yunnan provinces and their adjacent areas, covering one quarter of China's land area. The population distribution pattern of China's ethnic groups has been formed through long-term ethnic assimilation, in which some ethnic groups live together over vast areas while some live in compact communities in small areas. It is natural for an ethnic group to be distributed in various administrative regions, which is also the main feature and advantage of China's ethnic relations. The so-called "Greater Tibet" does not hold water either in history or in reality, and is completely against the trend of China's ethnic development. If the 55 minority ethnic groups established their own autonomous regions divided by ethnic groups, it would definitely obstruct the economic and cultural prosperity of minority ethnic groups and ethnic areas, and lead to ethnic disputes and social chaos in China that would jeopardize the country's stability and unification.

Fourth, the statements demand the central government to withdraw troops from "Greater Tibet." The 14th Dalai Lama said in the "Five-Point Peace Plan" that "only a withdrawal of Chinese troops could start a genuine process of reconciliation," and in the "Seven-Point New Suggestions" that "a regional peace conference should be called to ensure that Tibet becomes a genuine sanctuary of peace through demilitarization." As is known to all, a country maintains troops within its own territory not only out of consideration for international security but also as a symbol of national sovereignty. A withdrawal of troops from its own territory and transfer of that territory to be discussed by an international conference for the purpose of turning it into a "peace zone" cannot be agreed to by any government insisting on national sovereignty and dignity.

Fifth, the statements require non-Tibetans to move out of

"Greater Tibet." The 14th Dalai Lama said that "it is imperative that the population transfer is stopped and Chinese settlers return to China." The "Chinese settlers" he mentioned not only refers to the Han people but all non-Tibetan ethnic groups. The so-called "Greater Tibet" has been inhabited by a large number of ethnic groups for generations. The 14th Dalai Lama's call for the millions of Han, Hui and Mongolian people to move out of their home areas is actually an "ethnic cleansing" policy. Since the early 20th century, this policy has already plunged the peoples of a number of countries into an abyss of untold suffering.

Therefore, while the Dalai Lama claims to "seek solutions within the framework of the Constitution of China" his demands violate China's Constitution. The "genuine autonomy" he seeks is only one step away from "Tibet independence." The "middle way" advocated by the Dalai clique is a denial of the fact that Tibet has been an integral part of China ever since ancient times. It attempts to overthrow the leadership of the Communist Party of China in Tibet and other Tibetan areas, subvert the people's democratic politics, and undermine China's regional ethnic autonomy system, and set up a "semi-independent" political entity led by the Dalai clique to pave the way for the final realization of the "Independence of Greater Tibet."

125. In recent years the 14th Dalai Lama has stated that he may choose his own reincarnation while he is still alive, that his next reincarnation may be found outside China, and that he could halt his reincarnation. What do you think about these statements?

The reincarnation system for Living Buddhas distinguishes Tibetan Buddhism from other forms of Buddhism. In 1793 the central government of the Qing Dynasty issued the Imperially Approved Ordinance for the More Efficient Governing of Tibet (29-Article). The Ordinance stipulates that the reincarnation of the various Living Buddhas must follow the procedure of "drawing lots from the golden urn" under the supervision of the Qing High Commissioners, and the selected candidate would be confirmed and approved by the central government. Since then, it has become a religious ritual and historical convention. The 14th Dalai Lama's absurd assertions defy historical convention and the religious stipulations of Tibetan Buddhism. In fact, these assertions are aimed at seizing the power to confirm and guide the Dalai Lama's reincarnation from the central government. His purpose is to find a new leader for the so-called "Tibet independence" cause. This is evidence that the Dalai clique is distorting the tenets of Tibetan Buddhism to split China.

It is a trick of the 14th Dalai Lama to use religion as a tool for his political purposes. In recent years, he has done many things that went against Tibetan Buddhism and destroyed the normal order of this religion, as he attempted to undermine the stability of Tibet and seek "Tibet independence." For instance, he disregarded the historical convention and religious ritual of Tibetan Buddhism when he claimed to have identified, without the approval of the Chinese government, the so-called "reincarnated soul boy of the Panchen Erdini" from overseas, creating conflicts inside Tibetan Buddhist circle and persecuting the followers of the Dorje Shugden (Living Buddha of Dharma Protector). For the 14th Dalai Lama, religion is far more than a belief; it is also a mask and tool for his "Tibet independence" activities.

The Chinese government will, as always, respect history and religion, observe relevant laws and regulations, and try to find and confirm reincarnated soul boys for the Living Buddhas in line with the relevant historical convention and religious ritual of Tibetan Buddhism.

126. Why did the 14th Dalai Lama ban the worship of the Dorje Shugden?

The 14th Dalai Lama claims in foreign countries that he upholds equality between religions and different schools, and adheres to democracy, freedom and equality, thereby winning such titles as a "defender of human rights" and "messenger of peace." But in fact he carries out dictatorial policies inside the Tibetan Buddhist circle. One example of this is that in 1996 he announced that the Dorje Shugden was "an evil spirit" detrimental to the cause of a free Tibet, and so he inspired his "government in exile" to ban the worship of the Dorje Shugden. He has said on many occasions that the Dorje Shugden is pro-Han and harmful to the health of the Dalai Lama and to his "government in exile;" he also compiles materials which distort history and fabricate lies about the Dorje Shugden and has them printed and distributed among the Tibetans. Using the issue of the Dorje Shugden, he cheats some Tibetans and forces them to give up or convert to his own school. He instigates the "Tibetan Youth Congress" and "Tibetan Women's Association" and some other organizations for the independence of Tibet to smash the Dorje Shugden statues, attack monasteries that revere the Dorje Shugden and prosecute his followers, causing chaos and sowing discord between the Tibetan and Han people. Such activities have aroused strong opposition from monks and other Tibetans living overseas. Despite pressure from the Dalai clique, they refuse to convert to another religious belief and protest that the 14th Dalai Lama is "seeking religious hegemony," "depriving individuals of freedom of belief" and "ignoring history and violating justice." The persecution of the Dorje Shugden's followers reveals just how hypocritical this clique is.

127. What does the religious community of Tibet think about the 14th Dalai Lama?

After the March 14 riot in Lhasa, some venerable people in the Tibetan Buddhism community commented that what the 14th Dalai Lama had done violated the basic doctrine and disciplines of Buddhism, seriously breached the normal order of Tibetan Buddhism, defamed the good reputation of Tibetan Buddhism, and revealed his own hypocrisy.

According to Living Buddha Tsemon Ling TenzinTrinley, vice-chairman of the Chinese Buddhist Association, "*Karunapramana* (infinite pity for all beings)" is the essence of Buddhism, while "doing no harm to all beings" is the root of Buddhist doctrine. However, over the years, the Dalai clique has instigated a number of riots in Tibet and done other things to disrupt the normal order of Tibetan Buddhism in order to seek "Tibet independence." During the March 14 riot, premeditated and instigated by the Dalai clique, 18 innocent people were burned or hacked to death. Did the Dalai clique think of the essence of Buddhism or the root of Buddhist doctrine when they planned the riot? They have none of the "compassion, benevolence and pity" that are integral parts of true Buddhists.

As Living Buddha Shingtsa Tenzinchodrak once said, Sakyamuni Buddha requires Buddhists to pursue Buddhahood and not to intervene in state affairs. However, since fleeing China in 1959, the 14th Dalai Lama has never given up his political fantasy of splitting China and seeking "Tibet independence." Consequently, he has constantly created trouble over the so-called "Tibet question" in international relations. His seeking political power under the cover of religion does not conform to Buddhist doctrine.

According to Living Buddha Nye Ta of the Bon (the native Tibetan religion), in 1995 the Central Government of China searched for the reincarnated soul boy of the 10th Panchen Erdini according to religious ritual and historical convention. At that time the 14th Dalai Lama was in exile and could not himself search for the soul boy. Nevertheless, he announced that he had identified the reincarnated "soul boy" of the 10th Panchen, trying to deceive the public, but undermining the great event of the Living Buddha reincarnation. His act violated religious ritual and historical convention, and was against "the five commandments," "ten virtues" and some other Buddhist precepts.

128. How many times have the central government departments contacted the 14th Dalai Lama's representative? Why has there been no progress to speak of?

Since the 14th Dalai Lama fled to India in 1959 the central government of China has been patient with him and taken a stand favorable for safeguarding the country's unity and ethnic harmony. His post as a vice-chairman of the NPC Standing Committee was preserved until 1964.

In December 1978 Deng Xiaoping told an AP reporter: "The Dalai Lama may come back, but in his capacity as a Chinese citizen. We have only one demand – that he be patriotic – and we are adamant that there is no major difference as to when he becomes patriotic, sooner or later." His words expressed the central government's stand.

In 1979 the 14th Dalai Lama sent his private representative to China for the first time. At a meeting with the private representative, Deng Xiaoping said, "The fundamental problem lies in the fact that Tibet is part of China. It is the yardstick to judge whether things go right or wrong."

Since then, the central government departments have received over 20 groups of Tibetans from abroad who had close relations with the 14th Dalai Lama, including most of his relatives. His elder brother Gyalo Thondup has come back to China a dozen times for visits or negotiations with the central government departments. From 2002 to 2010, the central government of China arranged many visits for and talks with Lodi Gyari and some other Tibetans having close relations with the 14th Dalai Lama.

During these visits and talks, these people said they would inform the 14th Dalai Lama and other people of the status quo in China. Moreover, they expressed disagreement with the untrue statements about Tibet made by some people abroad. However, the overseas separatist forces have never stopped their activities.

In 2008, before the Beijing Olympic Games was held, during a meeting with the Dalai Lama's representatives Lodi Gyari and Kelsang Gyaltsen, Du Qinglin, vice-chairman of the National Committee of the Chinese People's Political Consultative Conference and minister of the United Front Work Department of the CPC Central Committee, pointed out that the Dalai Lama should openly and explicitly promise and prove by his actions that he would not support activities disturbing the upcoming Beijing Olympics or support plots to fan violent criminal activities, but that he would curb the violent terrorist activities of the "Tibetan Youth Congress" and not support any argument or activity aimed at seeking "Tibet independence" and splitting the region from the country. These representatives made such commitments at that time, but did not live up to them. Only a few days before August 8, the date of the opening ceremony of the Beijing Olympics, and several days thereafter, the 14th Dalai Lama organized over 16,000 person-times to make many troubles in front of over 40 Chinese embassies in foreign countries, disturbing the normal work of these embassies and threatening their staff and property. In the meantime, he instigated foreigners to make trouble around Olympic venues and Tiananmen Square. In later talks, he submitted to the central government a "memorandum" which advocated "Greater Tibet" with "high-level autonomy."

During its contacts and talks with the 14th Dalai Lama, the central government of China has kept to the principle that state unity, territorial integrity and national dignity are in the overriding interests of the Chinese people, and will never yield to anyone anywhere or at any time on these issues. The central government has always kept the door open to the 14th Dalai Lama as long as he adheres to patriotism, but has never and will never discuss the "independence," "semi-independence" or "independence in disguise" of Tibet.

The central government's nearly 30 years of contacts with the 14th Dalai Lama shows clearly that: (1) The Dalai Lama kept readjusting his strategy but has never given up his stand on "Tibet independence" or "independence in disguise." Although he changed his tone in the 1990s and proposed some suggestions and opinions for the solution of the Tibet question, these proposals all deny that Tibet has been an integral part of China since ancient times, ignore the people's government system with the people as the masters and the system of regional ethnic autonomy that all ethnic groups in Tibet have established under the leadership of the Communist Party of China. They make detours all the time around the concepts of "Tibet independence" and "Greater Tibet with high-level autonomy." (2) He keeps readjusting his strategy and tries to manipulate public opinion in the world by use of talks, severing contact with the central government when he thinks the international and Chinese situation is good for him, while demanding talks when he thinks the situation is not favorable for him. (3) Even while calling for contact with the central government of China, the Dalai Lama does not stop his separatist activities in China and abroad.

The above facts show that the central government of China has made every effort to bring about contacts and talks with the Dalai Lama, showing full sincerity. The reason that contacts and talks in the past reached no result was all because of the 14th Dalai Lama.

The central government still hopes that the 14th Dalai Lama can face up to history and reality, profoundly ponder his political stand, give up his demand for "Tibet independence," "semi-independence" or "independence in disguise," size up the situation, and make a correct decision by doing something good for the Tibetan people in his remaining years.

129. What is the attitude of the central government of China toward the contacts and talks with the 14th Dalai Lama?

The Chinese government's policy toward the 14th Dalai Lama has always been consistent and explicit. That is, we always keep the door open for contact between the central government and the 14th Dalai Lama, as long as he gives up his demand for "Tibet independence," stops separatist activities, and acknowledges publicly that Tibet and Taiwan are both inalienable parts of Chinese territory.

The central government has always kept contact with the 14th Dalai Lama with maximum sincerity and great patience. Since 1979 the central government departments have received more than 20 groups of the Dalai Lama's representatives and others visiting groups, including the close relatives of the Dalai Lama. However, no progress has been made during these contacts and talks, primarily because the Dalai Lama has no sincerity, never gives up his demand for "Tibet independence," nor stops separatist activities. In particular, from March 2008 the Dalai clique instigated a series of violent incidents in Tibet's capital of Lhasa and some other Tibetan-inhabited areas. Some of the rioters attacked Chinese embassies in foreign countries and tried to disturb the Beijing Olympic Games by different means. These acts undermined the basic principles and environ-ment necessary for meaningful contacts and talks between the central government and the 14th Dalai Lama.

Even so, we still keep the door open to the 14th Dalai Lama for further dialogue. The Dalai clique must stop instigating vio-lent crimes and separatist activities, and create a favorable envi-ronment and foundation for contacts and talks. In the meantime, we firmly safeguard the unity of the state, territorial integrity and national unity and protect the rights, life and property of the ordinary people of Tibet who used to be serfs and slaves, as the masters of the country.

130. The central government and the 14th Dalai Lama have failed to reach agreement. Will they continue their contacts?

In order to express respect for Tibetan Buddhism and its followers, the central government has made many contacts with the 14th Dalai Lama. But it has never recognized the so-called "Tibetan government in exile," so it only has contacts with the personal representatives of the 14th Dalai Lama.

The relevant departments of the central government keep the channels of contact with the 14th Dalai Lama open. It is hoped that contacts can help the 14th Dalai Lama know the actual conditions of the country, and have a clear understanding of the situation and the central government's policy toward the 14th Dalai Lama and other overseas Tibetans. The 14th Dalai Lama should show his sincerity, let his actions match his words, and avoid setting up new obstacles for the contact.

131. Some people in Western countries think the Chinese government delays the contact with Dalai Lama and avoids any "substantial negotiations" on "Tibet issue." Is that true?

After the 14th Dalai Lama fled abroad in 1959, in order to maintain the integrity of the country and the unity of all ethnic groups, China's central government was patient towards him and kept his post as the vice-chairman of the National People's Congress open till 1964. In 1979, for the first time, he sent a personal representative back to China. When meeting the representative, Deng Xiaoping pointed out, "The primary question is whether Tibet is a part of China or not. This is the standard to judge right and wrong." Since 1979 relevant departments of the Chinese government have received over 20 overseas Tibetan groups who were close to the 14th Dalai Lama, including his eldest brother, second brother, younger brother and sister.

However, the Dalai clique didn't respond to the central government's kindness positively; especially in the 1980s, some took advantage of their visits to Tibet to publicize secessionism, hold anti-government activities, and plot and participate in a riot in Lhasa. Under such circumstances, the central government still approved many times the visits by the 14th Dalai Lama's representatives for communication, and invited the 14th Dalai Lama in 1989 to return to Beijing to attend the funeral ceremony of the 10th Panchen Erdini. But he refused. Based on a wrong judgment of the situation, the Dalai side announced in 1993 that it wouldn't contact the "unstable Chinese government," and blocked the established channel of contact. Later, as China's national strength and international status kept growing, the Dalai side proposed to resume the contact with the central government, but they still refused to give a complete and positive response to the central government's principle and stand. They ignored the tremendous development in Tibet in the past decades, and continued to criticize and attack China's Tibet policy. The "Tibetan government in exile" with the 14th Dalai Lama as its head, repeatedly organized anti-China activities among overseas Tibetans, interfered with Chinese leaders' state visits to foreign countries, attacked Chinese embassies and consulates, persisted in demanding "Tibet independence," and planned various activities aimed at hampering the Beijing Olympic Games.

The aforementioned facts prove that the major reason why the contacts between the Central Government and the 14th Dalai Lama have made no progress is because the 14th Dalai Lama and his clique refuse to give up their stand for "Tibet independence" and stop separatist activities.

It is hoped that the 14th Dalai Lama will clearly understand the situation, give up his stand of "Tibet independence," and do something beneficial for the progress of the country and the Tibetan region in his remaining years.

132. What is the biggest obstacle in the negotiations between the central government and the 14th Dalai Lama?

The central government's policy towards the 14th Dalai Lama is consistent and clear. The door for negotiations is always open, as is the channel. But the 14th Dalai Lama has refused to give up his stand for "Tibet independence" and persisted in his political demand of "independence in disguise" and "semi-independence." Any progress in negotiations will depend on the 14th Dalai Lama's complete reconsideration and change of his political stand. The Dalai clique must stop all separatist and violent activities, and make positive efforts to improve its relationship with the central government.

133. The 14th Dalai Lama claimed on many occasions that the Chinese leaders were well aware of his disagreement with separatism, but it is more beneficial to the Chinese leaders by claiming that the Dalai Lama wants "Tibet independence." Is that true? Why does the Chinese government insist that the 14th Dalai Lama hasn't given up his demand for "Tibet independence"?

Wu Weiqun, executive vice-minister of the United Front Work Department of the CPC Central Committee, refuted that claim in a solemn statement through the media: It is nonsense, totally twisting the truth. The Dalai clique attempts to attract international attention by cooking up stories.

Regional ethnic autonomy is a basic political system of China, stipulated in its Constitution. The four-decade practice of the Tibet Autonomous Region since its founding has proved that such a system can guarantee that the country's ethnic minorities are their own masters, can greatly boost the overall social and economic development of the autonomous regions, and can effectively protect all the legal rights of ethnic minorities, including their right to use and develop their own spoken and written languages, and their right to maintain and develop their ethnic culture, as well as their freedom of religious belief. Conforming to Tibet's reality and fully welcomed by the Tibetan people, the system has set deep roots in Tibet.

The 14th Dalai Lama's so-called "high degree of autonomy" does not recognize the historical fact that Tibet has been part of China since ancient times, and does not accord with the present socialist system of Tibet. His demand for the Chinese army and the Han and other ethnic minority peoples to leave Tibet, and turn Tibet into an "international peace region" is totally unreasonable and unacceptable. The Chinese government's white paper *Regional Ethnic Autonomy in Tibet*, issued in 2004, clearly pointed out: The possibility of implementing another social system does not exist, because the situation in Tibet is entirely different from that in Hong Kong and Macao. The establishment of the Tibet Autonomous Region and the scope of its area are based on the provisions of the Constitution, and the laws on regional ethnic autonomy and decided by the conditions past and present. Any act aimed at undermining and changing regional ethnic autonomy in Tibet is in violation of the Constitution and law, and it is unacceptable to the entire Chinese people, including the broad masses of the Tibetan people.

The central government's policy as regards the 14th Dalai Lama is consistent and clear. It can have contacts with the 14th Dalai Lama and discuss his personal future as long as he admits publicly that Tibet is an integral part of China, truly gives up his stand of separatism, stops all separatist activities, and admits that Taiwan is an inalienable part of China. However, the 14th Dalai Lama has never done so; he insists on his wrong stand with the excuse of "a high degree of autonomy." The illegal "Tibetan government in exile" with him as the head is still employing people overseas to engage in separatist activities. The time is advancing; Tibet is progressing. It is hoped that the 14th Dalai Lama will make a correct judgment of the situation, truly and not simply verbally relinquish his insistence on "Tibet independence," and do something beneficial for the progress of China and Tibetan region in his remaining years.

134. What is the scope of the so-called "Greater Ti-
     bet region" insisted on by the 14th Dalai side
     in the negotiations and "memorandum"? Why
     does he insist on this?

The "Greater Tibet region" includes not only the Tibet Autonomous Region, but also the Tibetan-inhabited areas in Qinghai, Sichuan, Yunnan and Gansu provinces.

In spite of the historical facts and present-day reality,
the 14th Dalai Lama envisions all these places merging into a
"Greater Tibet region." He deliberately confuses the concept of
"Tibet" and the "Greater Tibet region," which has been inhabited by millions of the Han, Tibetan and other ethnic minority
peoples for long period of time. His purpose is to warp public
opinion.

135. What is the essence of the "genuine autonomy," "a high degree of autonomy," and "one country, two systems" proposed by the 14th Dalai Lama in his negotiations with the central government?

Regional ethnic autonomy is a basic political system stipulated in the Constitution, which has proved to be successful. The Tibet Autonomous Region was founded in 1965, and practices its autonomy rights in accordance with the law. The 14th Dalai Lama has concocted a "Greater Tibet region" that has never existed in history and isn't possible today either. His primary purpose is to negate China's present social system, and lay basis for his "Tibet independence."

"One country, two systems" is the fundamental principle of the central government to deal with the Hong Kong, Macau and Taiwan issues for the reunification of China. The situation in Tibet is entirely different from that in Hong Kong and Macao. The Hong Kong and Macao issue was a product of imperialist aggression against China; it was an issue of China's resumption of exercise of its sovereignty. Tibet, on the other hand, has been an inseparable part of Chinese territory since ancient times, and the central government has always exercised effective sovereign jurisdiction over the region. So the issue of resuming exercise of sovereignty does not exist. Through the peaceful liberation of

Tibet in 1951, the Democratic Reform in 1959 and the establishment of the Tibet Autonomous Region in 1965, the political and economic foundation for Tibet to practice the socialist system has become increasingly solid. It is the Tibetan people's choice to follow the socialist road together with the other peoples of the country. The possibility of implementing "one country, two systems" in Tibet does not exist.

136. Why does the central government insist that the
     14th Dalai Lama admit that Taiwan is an alien-
     able part of Chinese territory? What is the con-
     nection between him and the Taiwan issue?

China's central government policy concerning the 14th Dalai Lama is consistent: The 14th Dalai Lama should renounces
his demand for "Tibet independence," stop his separatist activities and recognize Tibet as a part of China and Taiwan as a part
of China as well, and the government of the People's Republic of
China as the sole legitimate government representing the whole
of China. For many years the 14th Dalai Lama has had links to
Taiwan separatists, working together to split the country. It is a
basic political requirement for the 14th Dalai Lama to admit that
Taiwan is an inseparable part of China.

137. Some people in the West think that the Chinese government is not sincere in stating its willingness to have contacts with the 14th Dalai Lama, as it and its media have never stopped criticizing the Dalai clique. Isn't this self-contradictory?

The Dalai clique has carried out many separatist activities that harm China's national unity, including the March 14 Incident and the violence during the Olympic torch relay internationally. They deserve to be criticized and condemned. The media expressed the voices of the Chinese people. It was hoped that, hearing the people's voices, the 14th Dalai Lama would be alarmed, change his position, and effectively stop planning and instigating separatist and violent activities, thus creating the conditions for further negotiations.

The contacts and negotiations between the relevant departments of the central government and the 14th Dalai Lama are internal affairs of China. The Chinese government consistently opposes any interference by foreign forces and any attempts to internationalize the Tibet issue.

138. If the Chinese government regards Tibet issue as entirely an internal affair of China, why does it inform other countries about its negotiations with the 14th Dalai Lama?

Tibet is a part of China, and Tibet issue is an internal affair of China. These facts are acknowledged by most countries. In fact, no country in the world regards Tibet as an independent country. Nevertheless, the Chinese government understand the concerns about Tibet affairs in international circles. The Chinese government informs the outside world about the situation of the negotiations, and lets them know China's stand and position. This is an effort the Chinese government makes to strengthen cooperation and communications with foreign countries, and also accords with international conventions. But the Chinese government firmly opposes any country using the so-called "Tibet issue" to intervene in China's internal affairs, which will send the wrong signal to the Dalai clique.

139. Some countries' leaders have stated that they would like to provide help for the negotiations between China's central government and the 14th Dalai Lama. How do you regard this?

The Chinese government has clearly announced that the negotiations with the 14th Dalai Lama are purely internal affairs of China. The door to contact with China's relevant departments is open and clear for the 14th Dalai Lama. The Chinese government hopes that the rest of the world will support its efforts to safeguard China's sovereignty, maintain its social stability and protect the interests of China's various ethnic groups.

The Violence in Lhasa on March 14, 2008

X

140. Some facts about the March 14 Incident
    —Was it a "peaceful demonstration"? And what
    measures did the Chinese government take to
    cope with the unrest?

The following facts will help readers to assess the nature of the March 14 Incident of 2008. On that day some monks and hooligans burned or otherwise destroyed 84 private vehicles and fire engines, seven schools, five medical establishments, 10 bank outlets, 908 shops and 120 residential houses. A total of 382 people were killed or injured, of whom 58 were seriously injured and 18 were hacked or burned to death. One policeman lost his life, and 241 were seriously injured. The riot caused direct property losses totaling almost 250 million yuan. Meanwhile, in the Gannan Tibet Autonomous Prefecture in Gansu Province mobs attacked policemen and passers-by, injuring 94 people, of whom four were seriously injured, and causing direct property losses totaling 230 million yuan. These facts show that the March 14 Incident was not a "peaceful demonstration" but pure terrorism.

The local police forces extinguished fires, cleared blocked roads, and did their best to protect the victims of the mobs and property under attack. No antipersonnel weapons were used.

141. Who was the direct planner of the March 14 Incident?

It has emerged that the March 14 Lhasa riots were premeditated, planned and organized crimes instigated by the Dalai Lama and his followers as part of the so-called "Tibetan People's Uprising," announced in January 2008. The aim of this plot is to undermine the social stability of Tibet, and finally separate it from the rest of China. They took advantage of the upcoming Olympic Games to be hosted by Beijing in that year to launch this "uprising." On January 4, 2008, the "Tibetan Youth Congress" and four other Tibetan radical separatist organizations proposed the "Tibetan People's Uprising" online, and organized a "return march" of the Tibetan diaspora. They even claimed that they would "spare no blood or life for 'Tibet independence'." The "Speaker of the Tibetan Parliament" Karma Chophel said that, taking the opportunity of Beijing's hosting the Olympic Games, they would carry out a series of activities to pressure the Chinese government to solve the "Tibet Issue" in 2008 or the following two years. The Dalai Lama called the Olympic Games the last opportunity to achieve "the independence of Tibet." The public security organs in Tibet found that there was a close relationship between the Dalai Lama and his cohorts and the crimes in Lhasa on March 14.

142. What is the nature of the "Tibetan Youth Congress"? Was it connected with the March 14 Incident?

With around 30,000 members in its 70-odd branches overseas, the "Tibetan Youth Congress" (TYC), which advocates the "full independence of Tibet from China," was founded in 1970. It is the largest component of the Dalai Lama's separatist movement.

Although most of the Tibetan aristocracy in exile opposed the TYC in its preparatory period, it was supported by the Dalai Lama, who gave the organization its name. Since 1989 many core members of the TYC have become leaders of the "Tibetan government in exile." As of today, eight Kalons, or "ministers," of the "Tibetan government in exile" have TYC backgrounds, and 90% of the staff of the "government" come from the TYC.

The TYC planned and organized the Lhasa riot on March 14. When interviewed by journalists on July 3, 2003, Gaisang Puncog, former chairman of the TYC, said, "We can use any method to serve our cause, whether violent or non-violent." He also organized a six-month guerrilla warfare training course for TYC members. On January 4, 2008, the TYC, together with the "Tibetan Women's Association," the "Students for a Free Tibet," the "National Democratic Party of Tibet" and the "GuChuSum

Movement of Tibet," announced the formation of the "Tibetan People's Uprising," which they called "a great turning point in the history of the Tibetan freedom movement." An ad hoc preparatory committee with Tsewang Rinzin, the head of the TYC, acting as its top leader, was organized to take charge of the coordination work and collection of funds. The "Uprising" was divided into four phases: first, shaping public opinion and recruiting members; second, instigating various incidents around the world from March 10, 2008; third, coordinated activities, mainly worldwide protests against China; fourth, causing unrest inside Tibet and in other parts of China. On March 15, the day following the March 14 Incident, the TYC convened a working committee conference in Dharamsala, India, which approved a resolution to "organize a guerrilla force to enter China for armed struggle." A preliminary plan was drawn up for recruiting personnel, raising funds and purchasing of weapons, etc. They prepared to secretly enter Tibet across the China-Nepal border, and "sacrifice at least 100 lives of Tibetans for victory."

143. Why should the 14th Dalai Lama take the responsibility for the March 14 Incident?

The 14th Dalai Lama and his followers, as well as the leaders of the TYC and the "Tibetan Parliament in exile", have declared in recent statements that a series of large-scale "peaceful uprisings" in Tibet since March 10, 2008 were struggles under the rightful leadership of the Dalai Lama, and a "supreme commanding commission" was set up to direct all the activities of the "Tibetan diasporas." In fact, the Dalai Lama tried to pressure the Chinese government in 2007, saying that "violent incidents" could take place in Tibet, and if the "Tibet issue" wasn't solved before the Olympic Games, a large-scale protest on March 10, 2008 would happen. In an interview with BBC on March 16, the Dalai Lama refused to agree to persuade the "protesters" to refrain from violent crimes. He claimed that he had not predicted that the protest would get out of control and develop into a violent incident. But, as the top leader of the so-called "Tibetan government in exile," he cannot avoid the responsibility for what has happened. And the victims of the riot and their relatives will never tolerate his role in the incident nor forgive him. He must take the responsibility for it.

144. What losses did the incident bring to the country and people?

Besides 382 citizens and 242 policemen injured or killed, as well as direct property losses of 250 million yuan, the March 14 Incident also caused serious damage to Tibet's tourism and retail industries. Because of the incident, the number of domestic and overseas tourists to Tibet in March 2008 dwindled to 14,200, a decrease of 48.7% over the same period of 2007. There were also few tourists in April and May, the busiest tourism season in Tibet. But as social order returned to Tibet the number of tourists started to increase again, reaching 96,000 in June, 350,000 in July, 460,000 in August and 550,000 in September that year. The total number of tourists in the third quarter of 2008 was 1.36 million. During the National Day Holiday week from October 1 to 7 the Tibet Autonomous Region received 257,000 tourists, and the region's tourism income was 81.49 million yuan.

145. What has been the relationship between the Han and Tibetan ethnic groups in Tibet since the March 14 Incident?

Tibetan and other ethnic minorities account for 95% of the total population of the Tibet Autonomous Region. Over 40 ethnic groups live together in this vast area. They care for and help each other on an equal footing, having formed a relationship of common prosperity through joint efforts. As is well known, the violent crimes in Lhasa on March 14, 2008 were premeditated, planned and organized by the Dalai Lama and his followers, supported and instigated by Western anti-China forces. All ethnic groups in Tibet were appalled at the mob violence, as they all suffered from it. Through the incident, peoples of all ethnic groups in Tibet got a deeper understanding that "having a united and stable society is happiness, and misfortunes come with a state of separation and unrest," and will thus more firmly support and maintain the integrity of the country and the unity of its ethnic groups, and oppose separatism.

146. How many people were arrested in the March 14 Incident? How many received jail sentences, and how many received death penalty? How many are still jailed, and how many have been released? Were any prisoners tortured?

The public security organ of Tibet arrested and detained 953 suspects after the March 14 Incident. Through legal procedures, 84 were sentenced by the courts of Tibet, among whom two received the death penalty and three were sentenced to death with a two-year reprieve. The rest have all been released after being punished and educated.

The judicial organs of the Tibet Autonomous Region interrogated the suspects in accordance with legal procedures. On the basis of justice and nonviolence, the basic principle was to educate the majority and punish the minority. All rights that the defendants should enjoy according to the law were guaranteed, and interpreters were provided for those who needed them.

Reference:

Violent crimes, including beating, smashing, looting and arson, took place in some areas in Lhasa and Taktse County on March 14 and 15, 2008, including the burning of 12 innocent people to death and the burning of six shops to the ground. These crimes brought huge losses of life and property, and damaged social order, security and stability. The Intermediate People's

Court of Lhasa heard the cases and announced the verdicts to the public on April 8 and 21. The *Tibet Daily* also made the details of the cases clear to the public through its reports on April 9 and 22, 2009.

During the hearings of the cases, the judicial organs of the Tibet Autonomous Region insisted on the policy of tampering toughness with gentleness, and "strictly controlling and discreetly considering the application of death penalty." The hearings and verdict announcements were made public in accordance with the relevant laws and regulations of the State. The litigation rights of defendants were completely guaranteed, and their national customs and dignity were respected. Criminal defense lawyers hired by themselves or public defenders who were assigned by the court in accordance with the law if they hadn't hired any themselves, gave complete defendant statements. Interpreters were also provided for the defendants.

147. Were the temples in Tibet cleared after the March 14 Incident?

Certain monks were instigated by the Dalai Lama and his followers to cause the unrest in Tibet, breaking the law, seriously violating the normal order in temples and badly damaging the images of monks who should cultivate themselves to be kind. Most of these monks who caused the unrest, however, were strangers with ulterior motivates and had not registered themselves with the temples, and were later educated and asked to leave by the religious authorities.

图书在版编目（CIP）数据

西藏知识问题解答：英文／王晨，董云虎主编；中华人民共和国
国务院新闻办公室编．—北京：外文出版社，2011
　　ISBN 978-7-119-07015-5

　　Ⅰ．①西… Ⅱ．①王… ②董… ③国… Ⅲ．①西藏－概况－英文
Ⅳ．① K927.5

　　中国版本图书馆 CIP 数据核字 (2011) 第 075313 号

责任编辑： 李　芳
英文翻译： 李　洋　王　玮　姜晓宁　刘奎娟　陈传林
　　　　　　韩清月　严　晶　王　琴　冯　鑫　邢彬彬
英文审定： Paul White　王明杰　徐明强
装帧设计： 北京大盟文化艺术有限公司
制　　作： 北京维诺传媒文化有限公司
印刷监制： 韩少乙

西藏知识问题解答
主编：王　晨　董云虎

出版发行： 外文出版社有限责任公司
地址： 中国北京西城区百万庄大街 24 号　　　**邮政编码：** 100037
网址： http://www.flp.com.cn　　　　　　　**电子邮箱：** flp@cipg.org.cn
电话： 008610-68320579（总编室）
　　　　008610-68327750（版权部）
　　　　008610-68995852（发行部）
印刷： 北京昌平百善印刷厂
经销： 新华书店／外文书店
开本： 880mm×1230mm　1/32　**印张：** 11.75　**字数：** 200 千
版次： 2011 年 9 月第 1 版第 2 次印刷
书号： ISBN 978-7-119-07015-5
09800（英）（平装）